Praise for *From Hot Mess to Blessed*

From Hot Mess to Blessed is a courageous and masterful work that will disturb you in the best way. I stand in awe of Julie's honesty, vulnerability, determination, and obedience and how that all resulted in her providing us with an invaluable harvest of spiritual insights that will bring hope and healing to anyone wishing to deal with life's most difficult passages in a deeply meaningful, faith-filled way. This affirming message of God's presence and love in the thick of crisis, chaos, and loss is a must read and a gem to be treasured. Beyond inspiring.

—**Torry Martin**, author, *Of Moose and Men*

If you've ever thought you were too messed up to do anything important for God, read this book. Julie Gillies writes with vulnerability, honesty, and a deep commitment to helping women find answers in God's Word. If life has thrown you a few curves and you've wondered how to move forward with confident faith and renewed joy, this is the book for you. Read it for yourself and then take a group of friends through it. The study questions for each chapter will take you deeper into God's truth, and the list of scriptures at the end will give you solid footing for a life of blessing! I highly recommend this book!

—**Carol Kent**, speaker and author, *When I Lay My Isaac Down*

Julie Gillies writes in the fullness of grace and truth, and offers hope for any one wondering if they are too much of a mess for God to bother with. In *From Hot Mess to Blessed*, Julie peels back the lies to get to our hearts' greatest needs—and then introduces us to the One who can meet them completely. If I could put this book in the hands of every woman, I would. I would look her in the eyes and say, "Read this, believe it, and keep it handy for the rest of your life!"

—**Glynnis Whitwer**, author of 10 books, including *Doing Busy Better*, executive director of communications Proverbs 31 Ministries

Julie Gillies's *From Hot Mess to Blessed* is a masterpiece. The way Julie weaves together words to describe the internal world of the soul drew me right into her story. She put words to things I've felt and experienced but didn't know how to express. Julie's story is relevant to women from all walks and journeys. Her ability to connect with the reader will inspire, encourage, help them grow emotionally, and, most importantly, fall more in love with Jesus.

—**Julia Mateer**, author of *Life-Giving Leadership*

Julie's new book, *From Hot Mess to Blessed*, had me at hello! What woman cannot relate to being a hot mess at some point in her life? (Like maybe this morning!) From the title to the last page, Julie inspired me to wrestle with some conflicting and limiting beliefs in my life. She is not afraid to question how and why God allows tough life struggles while sharing her gift of transparency and a buoy of hope. Julie masterfully unpacks the boxes of her own heart's most vulnerable places as she simultaneously applies freshly woven examples from women of the Bible. She reminds her reader of the foundational truth that our only chance of moving from messed to blessed is on the back of Jesus. Julie reminds women "believing is daring, but if we dare to believe, we will be blessed among women!" *From Hot Mess to Blessed* is an inspirational adventure that will challenge readers to live full lives as blessed hot messes!

—**Pat Layton**, speaker, coach, and author of *Life Unstuck*

I've felt like a "hot mess" more than one time in my life, and I can tell you it's not pretty. When I picked up Julie's book and started reading, I began to see hope and how God's promises really do change everything. The more I read, the more I see how I can go *From Hot Mess to Blessed*. Thank you, Julie, for making something that seems so complicated very simple and filled with hope.

—**Monica Schmelter**, *Bridges* talk show host, and general manager, WHTN, Christian Television Network

If life and circumstances have left you feeling beaten down, unneeded, without purpose, and even hopeless, Julie's words and honest transparency will breathe fresh hope, inspiration, and joy back into your soul. You'll be inspired and motivated to not only begin believing in yourself again and how much God adores you but believing a powerful transformation is possible in your heart, mind, and life through Him.

—**Tracie Miles**, speaker and author with Proverbs 31 Ministries

The further I got into *From Hot Mess to Blessed*, the deeper the personal heart transformation, and I experienced a beautiful spiritual realignment. The extravagant love of the Father washed over me as I read and received His truths. Julie weaves Scripture throughout, confirming our identities. Julie's personal story is captivating and relatable. She makes us realize that we're not alone in our struggles, and that the kindness of the Father is readily accessible. This is a book you'll want to read and pass on.

—**Michelle Tellone Skorski**, pastor at The Front, and radio host TheJoyFM Network, KWND The Wind, 88.3 WAFJ, WLCQ and WYQQ

From

HOT MESS
to
Blessed

Julie K. Gillies

HARVEST HOUSE PUBLISHERS
EUGENE, OREGON

Cover by Bryce Williamson, Eugene, Oregon

Cover Image © hanohiki / iStock

Julie K. Gillies is represented by MacGregor Literary, Inc.

FROM HOT MESS TO BLESSED
Copyright © 2017 by Julie K. Gillies
Published by Harvest House Publishers
Eugene, Oregon 97402
www.harvesthousepublishers.com

ISBN 978-0-7369-6703-7 (pbk.)
ISBN 978-0-7369-6704-4 (eBook)

Library of Congress Cataloging-in-Publication Data
Names: Gillies, Julie K., author.
Title: From hot mess to blessed / Julie K. Gillies.
Description: Eugene Oregon : Harvest House Publishers, [2017] |
Identifiers: LCCN 2017001285 (print) | LCCN 2017022897 (ebook) | ISBN
    9780736967044 (ebook) | ISBN 9780736967037 (pbk.)
Subjects: LCSH: Christian women—Religious life. | Identity
    (Psychology)—Religious aspects—Christianity. | Change
    (Psychology)—Religious aspects—Christianity.
Classification: LCC BV4527 (ebook) | LCC BV4527 .G553 2017 (print) | DDC
    248.8/43—dc23
LC record available at https://lccn.loc.gov/2017001285

Printed in the United States of America

17 18 19 20 21 22 23 24 25 / VP-KBD / 10 9 8 7 6 5 4 3 2 1

To my gracious heavenly Father,
Who breathed fresh hope and stunning promises into my very being.
It is through You alone I have dared to believe.

Acknowledgments

A big, fat thank you to Harvest House Publishers, who challenged me to write this book: I am grateful you believed in me. Special thanks to Kathleen Kerr, editor extraordinaire and kind friend, who made my words more effective than they might have been. Thank you to my husband, Keith, for supporting me, praying for me, and bringing home dinner more nights than I can count. And huge thanks to my awesome Facebook prayer support team. Your prayers buoyed, strengthened, and enabled me. May the Lord pour out His abundant blessings on you all.

Contents

A Note to the Reader

Hi, I'm Julie. For as long as I can remember, I've been something of a hot mess. I've experienced a lot of heartache and caused plenty. I have demanded perfection yet offered none myself. I've stumbled, fallen, and wondered why on earth God puts up with the likes of me.

What I have discovered is that the finished work of the cross has changed everything. Christ's love, forgiveness, and power have utterly changed me and continue to change me. He has filled my heart with fresh, holy hope and enabled me to believe His promises. My fervent hope is to be less hot mess and more blessed. May the promises in this book offer the same hope to you.

This book includes Scripture references in the AMPC translation—the Amplified Bible Classic edition. It is a literal equivalent translation, and I love how this particular translation clarifies and amplifies key Hebrew and Greek words, which you will notice via parentheses and brackets. It allows the reader to more completely and clearly grasp word meanings and enjoy nuances understood in the original languages. For me, it is a fuller, richer Scripture experience. I hope you grow to love it as much as I do.

Introduction

I t's a compelling thought: God speaks jaw-dropping promises to His women, and if we dare to believe Him, we will be blessed.

Consider Mary, an average young woman living her quiet little life in Nazareth, tending to her family's chores while daydreaming about her recent engagement to Joseph. Suddenly, the angel Gabriel steps from the heavenly dimension onto her humble patch of earth and says something outrageous. He makes a promise that could never be fulfilled through mere human effort.

He declares the upcoming birth of a Savior—the long-awaited Messiah—through her, a virgin. He makes it clear that she is God's chosen vessel, and that through her the stunning plan of redemption will occur. And then Mary does something equally outrageous.

She believes.

In spite of her initial misgivings and not quite understanding how it will all work, she chooses to believe what God tells her. And history declares her blessed among women.

Meet the scripture where it all started. We find it in the first chapter of Luke. I call it every woman's verse:

> Blessed (happy, to be envied) is she who believed that there
> would be a fulfillment of the things that were spoken to her
> from the Lord (Luke 1:45 AMPC).

The same mighty God who created the majestic Himalayas and the magnificent Milky Way galaxy, who created lavender fields and cater-pillars that morph into multicolored butterflies, who created distinct snowflakes and every unique fingerprint and the intricate beauty and splendor of humanity itself, whispers to women's hearts. He whispers divine things—holy promises—that don't always make sense to our minds, but always stir our hearts.

God speaks. He gives the promise. And we believe. It sounds so simple, doesn't it?

And yet, believing God's promises is sometimes the hardest part. Believing is daring. Believing flies in the face of all we're experiencing. We feel uncertain, scared we're making it all up in our heads. Our faith feels woefully wobbly and feeble. But if we dare to believe, we will be blessed among women.

The Two Struggles Every Woman Experiences

> He came to her and said, Hail, O favored one [endued with grace]! The Lord is with you! Blessed (favored of God) are you before all other women! (Luke 1:28 AMPC).

As Gabriel greeted Mary that momentous day, her mind struggled. The angel's salutation flooded her with a plethora of emotions: She was troubled, disturbed, and confused not only by the angel's appearance, but at the angel's pronouncement of who she was.

Blessed?

Favored of God before all other women?

What?

Scripture records that Mary "was greatly troubled and disturbed and confused at what he said and kept revolving in her mind what such a greeting might mean" (Luke 1:29 AMPC). Mary's struggle is ours as well.

Our first struggle is to believe that we are who God says we are.

Mary's struggle to understand and believe who God clearly declared her to be is familiar territory to women. We grapple with our own self-image, battling the continual war within us to believe that we really are who God says we are. That in spite of how we feel about ourselves at any given moment (but in particular in those moments we consider ourselves failures on some level), we are not defined by that failure, our past, how we look, our family heritage, or our woefully wrong choices and myriad distressing inadequacies.

Could it be that Mary made a twofold discovery on that exceptional, holy occasion? That on the day the Lord sent an angel to announce His stunning plans, before she even heard the news that she would conceive and give birth to the holy child, Mary would first ponder and come to understand—and even accept—exactly how God saw her?

For some of us, the fresh, bold concept of embracing who God says we are is new ground. It feels surprising, and (unfortunately) maybe even slightly wrong. We're accustomed to living within the constraints of believing less of ourselves—that how we are is how we will always be. Our mother was moody, and we are too. Our father was short-tempered, and that's just the way our family is wired. The fact that we struggle with stubbornness, strife, feelings of inadequacy, or the ability to hold a grudge like nobody's business is simply a given—a family legacy like freckles or muscular legs or blue eyes.

We've accepted a lesser version of ourselves.

Yet Mary learned she was not only blessed, but that she had found free, spontaneous, absolute favor and loving-kindness with God. This magnificent truth made Mary's heart soar. It burst free from whatever inaccurate self-image she'd formerly held as she embraced God's view of her.

What if, like Mary, we pondered and then truly accepted and dared to believe that we are who God says we are? What if we really believed that we are favored? That we are beautiful (Song of Solomon 1:15), accepted (Ephesians 1:6), new creations (2 Corinthians 5:17), precious in His sight (Isaiah 43:4), really and unquestionably free (John 8:36), and chosen (John 15:16)?

Believing that we are who God says enables us to burst free from our inaccurate self-images. And our truth-grasping hearts will place us in the strongest possible position to believe when God then speaks promises to our hearts. A place of confidence. A place of boldness. A place of absolute trust and complete surrender. This is what I believe transpired with Mary.

Over time, as Mary heard many people exclaim and declare awesome words over Jesus concerning His future, she pondered and treasured those words in her heart (Luke 2:19). I believe Mary did the same with the angel Gabriel's surprising declaration of who she was. She took time to meditate on those beautiful words and came to the place where she knew her value and worth in God's eyes. She was able to accept and rest in God's promise because she first accepted and rested in who He said she was.

We would be wise to do the same by emulating Mary—keeping His truths about who we actually are in our hearts, thinking about them often, and allowing them to sink in. Heaven knows we engage in negative self-talk often enough. Why not turn that around and instead ponder God's truth about who He says we are? We are not only loved, accepted, capable, and chosen, we are His image bearers (Genesis 1:27), created to reflect God: His beauty, His light, His truth, His grace, His joy, His peace, His love. It's a beautiful twofold truth: When we truly know who we are, we more accurately reflect Whose we are.

The acceptance of who she was prepared Mary to receive the promise of what was to come—even when it appeared absolutely ridiculous. A virgin giving birth? Who had ever heard of such a thing?

Our second struggle is to believe the stunning promises He whispers to our hearts.

> You will conceive and give birth to a son, and you will name him Jesus. He will be very great and will be called the Son of the Most High. The Lord God will give him the throne of his ancestor David. And he will reign over Israel forever; his Kingdom will never end! (Luke 1:31-33).

Though Mary's heart thrilled at Gabriel's surprising announcement, she initially struggled to comprehend how on earth this (let's face it) slightly perplexing promise could actually transpire. I think that the Lord often leads us in ways we don't understand to give us the opportunity to trust Him in a bigger way and to believe Him in spite of how things appear.

Though Mary could have argued with the archangel, listing reason after reason why she could not possibly give birth or be used by God in such a spectacular way (how many times have we done that very thing—offering God our lists of why it won't work?), her heart was humble and obedient and willing.

> When we truly know who we are, we more accurately reflect Whose we are.

And there is nothing God cannot do when our hearts are humble, obedient, and willing. Those are priceless commodities in God's sight. In fact, God searches the earth for those with willing hearts. When we commit to His way and say yes, His Spirit immediately swoops in and strengthens us. God sees the holy determination and commitment in our hearts, even along with our fears, and He girds our hearts.

Mary chose to receive God's stunning promise; she just didn't know how, exactly, it would all work.

The Answer to *How*

Mary's stunning angelic encounter that day beat a holy cadence:
You have.
You are.
You will.
He will.

These spectacular proclamations penetrated Mary's heart. *You have found favor with God. You are blessed among women. You will conceive. Your child will be very great.*

In the midst of this jaw-dropping event, as Mary's heart soaked in every word, she struggled to understand how on earth this could possibly happen. Because it made no sense. She was a virgin. And Mary may have been innocent, but she was not stupid. She knew what pregnancy required. Scripture records that "Mary asked the angel, 'But how can this happen? I am a virgin'" (Luke 1:34).

How many times do we struggle because the very thing God is speaking to our hearts makes no sense to us? We wonder, *How? How can I lead a group when I've had no training? How can I start a business since I'm a busy wife and mother? How can I ask for forgiveness since the bridge is already burned? How can I buy a house since I'm a single mom? How can this happen since _____?*

Our human minds struggle to grasp God's infinite abilities. We struggle because our issues—the deep ones we wrestle with in private—seem impossible to overcome. We struggle because we are baffled by the logistics. We struggle because, though we desperately long to believe, so much of what we see is the exact opposite of the promise. Our hearts soak in the promise but cannot comprehend the how.

And finally, the unfathomable answer.

The Holy Spirit will.

It's how God accomplishes everything on earth: through and by the same Spirit Who hovered over the waters (Genesis 1:2), the same Spirit Who created all of humanity (Genesis 1:26), the same Spirit Who raised Christ from the dead.

That's exactly what the angel said to Mary:

> The Holy Spirit will come upon you, and the power of the Most High will overshadow you [like a shining cloud]; and so the holy (pure, sinless) Thing (Offspring) which shall be born *of you* will be called the Son of God (Luke 1:35 AMPC).

Essentially, Gabriel said, *The Holy Spirit will do, Mary, what only He can do. He will create and bring life. Let Him.* And that single revelation is why Mary was able to respond, surrender, accept, and yield to God's remarkable plan. *The Holy Spirit will.*

The same holds true for us.

When we don't know how, when we don't know what, when we don't know why…the answer is always, *The Holy Spirit will.* The Holy Spirit comes upon us, equips us, enables us, empowers us. He accomplishes His divine will and establishes God's perfect plans and purposes. He does what only He can do. He creates and brings life. He births holy things in us and through us…if we will yield to Him.

At some point, Mary's face must have appeared slightly confused because Gabriel continued speaking, underscoring God's mighty ability and banishing every last doubt from Mary's troubled mind. His words are some of the most powerful in the New Testament: "With God nothing is ever impossible and no word from God shall be without power or impossible of fulfillment" (Luke 1:37 AMPC).

What if we dared to believe that God could do anything—anything at all in and through us? What if, like Mary, our hearts were open in the midst of our most baffling, uncomfortable, unlikely situations?

Are we willing? Are we willing to believe God, not because we're equipped and ready and all our adorable, fluffy ducks are in a charming little row, but because He says we are, and because we trust that His strength is made perfect in weakness? If He is able, then what is holding back the hope He is offering to us?

A promise from the Lord is an invitation to enter into agreement with our Creator. With the One Who parted the Red Sea. With the One Who closed the mouths of lions. With the One Who is Faithful and True. When God sent the archangel Gabriel to deliver His message to Mary, it was an opportunity for her to participate in His specific plans for her *and* in what He was currently doing on the earth. A beautiful, holy meshing was about to take place between heaven and earth, and the Most High God was inviting her to participate and believe.

Entering into this agreement requires us to lay down our doubts, to surrender our need to completely understand how every minute detail is going to transpire, and to let go of our expectations of how things should go. It's a daring step through the sometimes scary door of promise. Not scary because we fear our heavenly Father, but scary because of what such a step demands of us. Courage. Faith. Moxie we're not sure we possess.

Yet when we surrender and believe, He beautifully weaves our small stories into His big, grand picture so that our lives beautifully reflect His amazing power and grace and love.

Today God is still speaking to His women wherever we are currently in life, offering promises of hope and a future (Jeremiah 29:11). He whispers words we long to hear. Words of unfathomable hope. He says to us, *If you will believe Me and cooperate with Me, I will birth great things in you and through you.*

> A promise from the Lord is an invitation to enter into agreement with our Creator.

God has unique and beautiful plans, dreams, and assignments for each one of us. We may not receive an archangel's visit, but He extends His holy invitation to every one of His women just the same. As God birthed the Messiah through Mary, His chosen vessel, so He births beautiful things through us. If we listen, what He speaks will resonate in our hearts. Not because it seems easy or likely or because it even makes sense initially. But because we sense that if we move forward into that promise, we will not only fulfill our own God-given destinies, but part of God's bigger picture on earth, as well.

And while Mary probably felt incredulous that God could accomplish such a miraculous event through her, it was His plan all along. He sees things in our hearts we don't even realize are there. It is God's good pleasure to show Himself strong in us and through us.

Years ago God whispered His promises to my hot mess of a heart, sparking divine hope. It seemed incredibly daring and often felt distinctly impossible that my deepest desires would unfold, but through tears and gritted teeth, I dared to believe.

And God moved.

God births supernatural things through women. He whispers to our imperfect hearts and beckons us to believe His stunning promises. Even when we're a hot mess. When we dare to believe Him, He is honored. He is glorified. And His promises begin to unfold.

What promises are you holding on to? Has God whispered a stunning promise to your heart—one so big there's no way it can be accomplished apart from Him? Or maybe you are gripped by the fear that there is no promise for you.

If you've ever felt like you're somewhere between a rock and a hot mess, you're not alone. And contrary to how it might seem, you're actually in a good place. A divine place. A place where holy promise exists. A place where every woman (and let's face it, each of us is one degree or another of a hot mess) can dare to believe and embrace *all* God offers.

1

And Then I Knew Normal Wasn't Out of the Question

I WILL MAKE YOU WHOLE

*What, what would have become of me] had I not believed that
I would see the Lord's goodness in the land of the living!*

PSALM 27:13 AMPC

When I first saw her, my jaw dropped. She stood in the middle of a weed-flanked dirt road a good quarter mile ahead of me. Sunlight in the eastern sky crowned her with glowing splendor. And when she turned around and smiled at me, her bright eyes radiated light and joy, emotional stability, and rock-solid confidence.

Envy tingled right up my spine. Every cell in my body longed to be like her.

But the truth was, I was nothing like that radiant woman. A perpetual cloud of anger hovered over me. A miserable heart etched my eyebrows into a semipermanent scowl. And insecurity punctuated every other sentence.

Yet as I sat in my worn prayer chair that morning, fervently praying, begging God to move in my life and to change me, that radiant woman is who I saw. And the crazy thing is, I knew that *she* was *me*. The future me. Crazy as it sounds, I was seeing my potential self way off down the road.

Back then I had no idea that "normal" was even remotely possible for me. I believed that I was the way I was, period. And though I prayed for God to move in my life, I didn't realize the depth to which He could transform a desperate, willing heart. I labeled myself as damaged goods, certain everyone saw the inner chaos and wounds that rendered me what I considered abnormal. And everything in me longed for normal. Well, *my* definition of normal, anyway: emotionally healthy, stable, and confident—for starters. As a new believer, I simply had no inkling that through Christ good, permanent change was possible.

Yet in that moment, I previewed staggering evidence of Jesus's amazing power to transform. I understood that I could choose His journey for me and wind up in that very place down the road. A beautiful place of joy, emotional health, and confidence in Christ. In His vast lovingkindness, God allowed me to glimpse the woman He created me to be so that my heart could catch hold of the potential He saw in me, and so that I would see a glimmer of hope for myself—hope for a normal life.

You know you are a hot mess when your goal is *normal*.

And though I couldn't have articulately defined normal at the time, I instinctively yearned for it. That single, sacred glimpse enabled my longing heart to perceive that through Christ my yearnings were attainable. That through the power of the One Who created me, I could be free of intense anger, stifling insecurity, crippling timidity, and crazy fear…and that's just the short list of the ugly that controlled me.

And then a strange thing happened.

As I grew closer to the Lord and He began a deep work, His light in my heart increased, which exposed more of my inner ugly. Initially, that didn't make sense. Yet I began to understand that He was exposing the darkness lurking in my heart, making me aware that when we are controlled by anything other than the Holy Spirit, we're actually enslaved. Deep down I didn't want to be angry or insecure or timid or afraid. But at various times, each of those emotions held me captive.

In 2 Peter 2:19, the apostle tells us, "You are a slave to whatever controls you." I didn't want to be a slave. I was weary of my wounded soul calling the shots. I wanted my soul fractures healed. I wanted the sweet breeze of freedom to blow across my heart, sweeping all the dark ugliness away with it. And if God's Word was true, then the freedom I read about was more than nicely phrased words on a page. Freedom was a promise—a tangible thing God could accomplish in me if I dared to believe. John 8:36 promises, "If the Son liberates you [makes you free men], then you are really and unquestionably free" (John 8:36 AMPC).

And so a holy promise was conceived in my heart that morning. The promise of how far God could take a woman if she dared to believe that He was greater than past hurts, past screwups, past foolish choices, and zero confidence; that He could somehow take all the fragments of a tragically broken heart and life and make them whole. It seemed outrageous to believe that a hot mess like me could be made whole, but everything in me ached to be *really and unquestionably free*.

Over the years I never forgot or let go of that sacred glimpse of the potential future me. I held on to it like an exhausted swimmer clings to a buoy. This precious promise infused into the very blood in my veins and wound round and round my circulatory system, regularly reminding me of God's good plans.

God had revealed His intended final outcome to me, and He offers the same to you.

> "I know the thoughts and plans that I have for you," says the Lord, "thoughts and plans for welfare and peace and not for evil, to give you hope in your final outcome" (Jeremiah 29:11 AMPC).

This is our amazing Father's heart toward us. He not only thinks of us, He has plans for us—for you—and they are good plans. Plans for freedom, plans for an abundant life, plans to make us more than conquerors over all that life throws at us, and plans to enable us to walk in the fullness of everything He declares over us, in spite of every outward obstacle and even the ugly things that lurk within us. He sees our full potential, and He challenges us to believe He can make us whole.

It doesn't matter if we can't figure out all the details and facts. Had Mary tried to figure out exactly how this supernatural Holy Spirit coming upon her thing was going to work, she could have thought herself right out of God's plans for her life. Sometimes all our thinking allows mere facts to supersede God's ability. Our minds rotate around and around the problem, which runs interference with our heart and faith. But we cannot allow ourselves to be sidetracked by mere facts. Mary didn't.

Instead, she dared to believe.

Initially, like Mary, I couldn't figure out how God would make it all happen. I had no clue how to get from where I was to where I saw the future me, but soon I understood that I didn't need to understand the intricacies. When our hearts sense a divine promise, we'd better believe that God can make it happen. Even when the details leave us befuddled. God isn't asking us to figure it out, plan it, or orchestrate it.

He is simply asking us to believe.

That very morning I made the decision that I would do whatever it took, and I would believe. I would cooperate with God's plans, His promptings, His discipline, and all His ways. I didn't care how long it took (though, of course, sooner would be better—much better), or what it cost me (and oh, it cost me!). Everything in me longed to be all that God created me to be and to accomplish all the things I sensed He had for me to do. I instinctively knew that somehow God could miraculously work and fulfill His promises.

The Glory of a Remodeled Life

If you've ever lived through a major remodeling project, you probably have a serious appreciation for the hard work involved in transforming a ramshackle house into a comfortable, beautiful place to live.

The way I see it, anyone can move into a brand-new house. Zero sweat equity. Instant pretty. But remodeling takes a willing investor with a keen eye for potential—someone prepared to put a lot of hard work into a far-from-perfect building. Done right, the results are a gorgeous old home with character, yet filled with all the new stuff you wouldn't want to live without. The before and after photos are remarkable, and no one who visits your house can believe that it ever looked like *that* before.

It's truly a labor of love.

My husband, Keith, and I were crazy enough to take on such an endeavor back when we were newly married, young, and willing to invest some serious elbow grease. We had purchased a tiny two-bedroom, one-bathroom, stinky, old, sorry excuse for a house, mostly because it only cost us $55,000.

Its flat, gravel-topped roof needed replacing, the jalousie windows had to go, the scary carpet reeked to high heaven, and the hot water heater needed to be moved out of the kitchen. Add in a garage, new electrical wiring, and paint—lots of paint—and it would be habitable.

Did I mention I was pregnant when we began?

We ended up knocking down walls and adding some extra rooms. It was almost a total do-over. For seven months, we stressed, sweated, and toiled, working far too hard and sleeping far too little. Then we watched in amazement and great satisfaction as our smelly, rinky-dink place was slowly shaped into something beautiful.

God does this very thing with us. He deeply values us, His daughters, and sees the potential that others (and often we ourselves) cannot. He deems us worthy of His investment. His Holy Spirit pinpoints areas in our hearts and lives that need loving restoration, and He gently coaxes us to believe, surrender, and cooperate with Him.

Some of us have sagging foundations. Some of us are a slapdash paint job on rotting boards. Some of us have broken windows where thieves can crawl in. All of us need a complete do-over. Like the hot water heater standing awkwardly in the middle of my kitchen, we often recognize when things are out of place. We know when parts of us are broken, and yet we aren't really sure how to change. We are powerless to make changes apart from Christ. As the psalmist puts it, "Unless the LORD builds a house, the work of the builders is wasted" (Psalm 127:1).

> He deems us worthy of His investment.

Unless we partner with God by surrendering to the work He is doing, cooperating with His promptings and discipline, and doing our part by saturating our hearts in His Word and spending time with Him in meaningful prayer, our house will remain in the same sagging, sorry shape.

He's willing. Are we? Are we willing to deny ourselves, pick up our crosses, and follow Him through the intimate intricacies of deep inner heart work? Will we submit ourselves, hearts wide open, to the One who is able to renew and restore? Because that is God's heart for us. He knows the things that have stripped us of our hope, our trust, our dignity. And He is well able to replace all the enemy has stolen from us (Joel 2:25). Jesus is willing to beautifully restore the years spent languishing in hurt, the broken areas we cover and attempt to hold together on our own, and the dreams we think are irretrievably dead.

Regardless of the degree of our need for a wise and loving Carpenter's skill, His purpose remains identical for each of us: wholeness. Part of the reason He does this is to demonstrate His willingness and ability to use broken, imperfect people, which more beautifully illustrates His greatness and power. We may struggle with both visible and invisible scars, but God doesn't always make them vanish. When our Savior rose from the grave, He not only still had scars, He pointed them out to those who doubted.

We don't have to be ashamed of our scars, for they point to a mighty Savior. He transforms our wounds into pinpoints through which His glorious light can gleam.

When we're tempted to believe our past is too much to overcome, we would be wise to take time to examine the Scriptures and learn about some of the people Jesus miraculously made whole:

- The paralyzed man (Matthew 9:2)
- The demoniac (Mark 5)
- The woman with the issue of blood (Luke 8)
- The man crippled for 38 years (John 5)
- The high priest's servant who had an ear cut off (John 18)

If Jesus miraculously moved in each of the lives represented above, He can do the same for us. This brief list hardly begins to cover the countless people whose lives Jesus lovingly restored. In fact, at the end of his Gospel, the apostle John declared, "Jesus also did many other things. If they were all written down, I suppose the whole world could not contain the books that would be written" (John 21:25).

Clearly, Jesus is serious about healing people. The ones who cry out to Him. The ones who know they are broken. The ones who desperately need freedom. If He restored each of *those* lives, and He is the same yesterday, today, and forever (see Hebrews 13:8), then we know He is *still* at work and eager to move in our lives too.

When we allow God to have His way by surrendering to His process, reading His Word and truly believing it, and investing in some serious prayer time, we will live an overcoming life—a life that is not held back by issues that once plagued us. Our lives will become testimonies to those around us. The more we allow Jesus to do in us, the more His glory is revealed. And that is His ultimate goal: a world full of regular people whose hearts and lives have been utterly transformed and radiate His unmistakable image.

Though it can be a long, arduous process, Jesus, with His keen eye, restores us to better than new. He makes us whole. We wind up beautiful, yet functional, and filled with His character. When we share our amazing before and after stories, no one can believe that we ever lived like *that* before because our hearts are all sparkly and fresh and new. It's truly a labor of love.

> He transforms our wounds into pinpoints through which His glorious light can gleam.

But there is always a price to pay.

It Always Costs Us More

God once gave me a wake-up call through an unusual fruit-filled dream. In my dream, as I searched through our refrigerator, I spotted a container of gorgeous red raspberries I thought my husband would love.

I walked over to the kitchen sink and began pouring the raspberries into the cupped palm of my hand, holding them under the faucet's cool stream of water. When I finished rinsing them, I released the berries into a clean bowl, only instead of tumbling into the bowl, several of the raspberries stuck to my hand. Painfully. In fact, the golden hairs on each berry, no longer soft and nearly invisible, had lengthened and hardened and now plunged into my palm like deep, wooden splinters.

Agony.

In excruciating slow motion, I began tugging each splinter from the swollen, tender palm of my hand. In my dream, my palm hurt so badly that I awoke, bolting straight up with my right hand extended.

God had my attention for sure.

At the time of this dream, my marriage was in a sorry state, my heart heavy and miserable. So that morning as I lay in bed praying about the dream's meaning, I felt shocked and slightly indignant about what I sensed God speaking to my heart.

God wanted me to offer my husband, Keith, fresh fruit. The fruit of love and patience and kindness and self-control. The fruit we both knew my husband rarely saw because I rarely offered it. If he was mean, so was I. If he was rude, then I was too. I spouted whatever I thought. I lived in self-defense mode, but God wanted me to change, and I sensed Him inviting me to walk differently, both with and in His Spirit.

> Walk and live [habitually] in the [Holy] Spirit [responsive to and controlled and guided by the Spirit]; then you will certainly not gratify the cravings and desires of the flesh (of human nature without God) (Galatians 5:16 AMPC).

For entirely too long I had allowed my sinful human nature to dominate my reactions in my marriage relationship. When my husband's words and actions hurt me, my reaction often gratified my flesh. And now God was asking me to change that. To do the right thing. Everything in me wanted to shout, "What about *him?*" And yet I couldn't escape the fact that *my* actions were wrong, and *my* actions were obviously what God was targeting here.

Resisting my bossy flesh would feel as painful as sharp wooden splinters piercing the palm of my hand. I knew it would be downright excruciating to keep my mouth closed when a stinging retort tingled on the tip of my tongue. And yet it seemed to be what God was requiring of me.

I had hoped and expected for God to change my husband, but

that wasn't happening. Yet. Instead, He wanted me to train myself to respond in a completely different way. His way.

Our Expectations

Naaman was a mighty man of valor and the commander of the king of Aram's army. Scripture says that "through him the LORD had given Aram great victories" (2 Kings 5:1). Naaman had high expectations for himself—expectations that were stalled when he fell ill with leprosy.

A young servant girl in his household convinced Naaman's wife that a prophet in Samaria could cure leprosy (2 Kings 5:2-3). Naaman eventually wound up at the home of Elisha, his hopes high. Yet, things didn't unfold the way Naaman anticipated.

> Naaman went with his horses and chariots and waited at the door of Elisha's house. But Elisha sent a messenger out to him with this message: "Go and wash yourself seven times in the Jordan River. Then your skin will be restored, and you will be healed of your leprosy" (2 Kings 5:9-10).

Naaman's highfalutin expectations didn't materialize. Accustomed to his commands being followed to the letter, the commander was indignant that Elisha didn't even bother coming to the door. And he was livid at being told to wash in a river that he considered beneath him and not nearly as good as the rivers of Damascus (2 Kings 5:12).

His outrage nearly cost him his healing.

This courageous commander was required to do something he clearly didn't want to do. He expected one thing but was told to do something else entirely. Seven times.

How many times has God asked us to do something we have no desire to do—the antithesis of our expectations—over and over?

Naaman believed the rivers of Damascus were better than all the waters in Israel (verse 12). In other words, he had a better idea, a superior way. Aren't we the same way? Don't we often attempt to manipulate things to go in accordance with our way of thinking, our ideas, and in our timing?

Naaman had a major heart change and finally relented. Dropping his expectations, dropping his armor on the riverbank, and dropping to his knees, he humbled himself. Realizing all he had to lose was his pride, he rose and entered the river, washing seven times. Not only did his skin become like that of a young child, but I believe his heart did too.

Dipping in the Jordan River wasn't what Naaman wanted or expected. And offering beautiful, costly fruit to my husband was not exactly what I wanted or expected either. But God's ways are not our ways (Isaiah 55:8), and the Lord requires us to do our part. There is no instant pretty. Only the high price of obedience, humbling ourselves, and willingly letting go of our expectations.

Only then does healing and wholeness happen.

When at last I humbled myself and began the painful, never-ending journey of relinquishing my expectations, and began sincerely making the effort to change the fruit I offered to my husband, healing began in me too.

It Usually Takes Longer Than We Want

The morning our teeny, stinky house remodeling project began, I bounced out of bed, elated. But as the work progressed on the same achingly slow timeline as my imperceptibly increasing stomach girth, frustration set my teeth on edge. Everything took four times as long as we thought. Piles of cement blocks littered our yard, construction workers' trash collected against our back fence, and ever-increasing layers of drywall dust coated everything we owned. My sense of humor evaporated right along with my privacy. What should have been an eight-week project snowballed into seven long months.

Did I mention our baby boy was born in the middle of it all? I arrived home from the hospital with Joshua three days post emergency C-section, greeted by construction workers and a lovely staccato hammer rhythm reverberating through our house.

It never seems to work out on our timetable, does it?

There are divine delays, and there are enemy tactics. It would behoove us to prayerfully discern between the two. And while that isn't always easy, when we ask the Lord for increased discernment, He enables us to understand the season and the culprit—whether it's the enemy or our own impatience. When we have at least a measure of understanding, we are far more likely to cooperate with and yield to the Lord's timing rather than interfere. This makes for a far more effective prayer life, enabling us to either pray against the schemes of the enemy ("…for we are familiar with his evil schemes"—2 Corinthians 2:11), or quiet our hearts and grow in patience and trust, all the while praying in alignment with God's will.

Consider Abraham's 25-year wait for God's promise of making this fatherless 75-year-old a great nation (Genesis 12). After waiting in expectation for a long 24 years, Abraham looked up, and the Lord appeared to him (Genesis 18:2).

> [The Lord] said, I will surely return to you when the season comes round, and behold, Sarah your wife will have a son (Genesis 18:10 AMPC).

I have discovered that God and I hold vastly different interpretations of "when the season comes round." My expectation leans more toward the immediate. In the meantime, more ugly oozes out of me, and I realize that if I trusted God on the level I claim I do, I wouldn't doubt, foam at the mouth with impatience, and feel frustrated that my plans aren't working out.

If we truly believe that our times are in His hands (see Psalm 31:15), then why do delays make us come so unglued?

And yet God, Who beautifully and seamlessly orchestrates the tides, the stars, the cycles of summer and winter, day and night, the God Who knows me far beyond my ability to know myself (I've never even attempted to count the number of hairs in my hairbrush, let alone on my head), surely has not forgotten me. And He has not forgotten you.

Though we may long for what we consider a more expedient unfolding of God's promises, when we yield to His ways, He enables us to see with eyes of faith. Abraham saw through these very eyes—eyes that saw not the circumstances before him, but the supernatural promise far ahead of him.

Abraham's focus was the key to his strong faith. Scripture records several specific times when Abraham looked up—key moments in his life where God enabled him to see the very thing that propelled him forward and strengthened his faith.

- On the third day of their journey, Abraham **looked up** and saw the place in the distance (Genesis 22:4).

- Then the LORD took Abram outside and said to him, "**Look up** into the sky and count the stars if you can. That's how many descendants you will have!" (Genesis 15:5).

- Then Abraham **looked up** and saw a ram caught by its horns in a thicket (Genesis 22:13).

- He **looked up** and noticed three men standing nearby (Genesis 18:2).

How many times do we keep our eyes glued to our circumstances, stuck on the very thing that keeps our hearts knotted? We focus on the situations or people, and we grow weary. We want to give up. Quit. Just forget the whole blasted thing.

When we choose to look up, we gain God's wisdom and understanding and truth, and we gain fresh perspective. The apostle Paul reminds us, "Let us not lose heart and grow weary and faint in acting nobly and doing right, for in due time and at the appointed season we shall reap, if we do not loosen and relax our courage and faint" (Galatians 6:9 AMPC).

At the appointed season. Do we trust God's timing? When we've prayed for years without seeing change, when we've cried out but heard nothing in response, when we feel like we cannot possibly hold on one moment longer and retain a smidgen of our sanity...how do we keep going?

The secret to not growing weary in well-doing is our focus. When we shift our focus, we look away from the multitude of things in our lives that distract us from His promise, that threaten His promise, that appear to override His promise, and gaze into the eyes of the Author and Finisher of our faith:

> Looking away [from all that will distract] to Jesus, Who
> is the Leader and the Source of our faith [giving the first
> incentive for our belief] and is also its Finisher [bringing
> it to maturity and perfection]. He, for the joy [of obtain-
> ing the prize] that was set before Him, endured the cross,
> despising and ignoring the shame, and is now seated at
> the right hand of the throne of God (Hebrews 12:2 AMPC).

When we look up as Abraham looked up, we see the holy possibilities, our faith and strength are renewed, and we are able to persevere,
even when it's taking far longer than we ever imagined.

Allowing Our Belief to Propel Us Toward Jesus

The bleeding woman understood what it meant to endure and persevere. For a miserable 12 years she bore an embarrassing, debilitating,
isolating disease (Mark 5:25-34).

The book of Leviticus illuminates the degree to which this woman
had suffered:

> If a woman has a flow of blood for many days that is unre-
> lated to her menstrual period, or if the blood continues
> beyond the normal period, she is ceremonially unclean. As
> during her menstrual period, the woman will be unclean
> as long as the discharge continues. Any bed she lies on and
> any object she sits on during that time will be unclean, just
> as during her normal menstrual period. If any of you touch
> these things, you will be ceremonially unclean. You must
> wash your clothes and bathe yourself in water, and you will
> remain unclean until evening (Leviticus 15:25-27).

The bleeding woman lived apart from her peers because anyone
who came into contact with her became ceremonially unclean. She
had limited interaction with her family for the same reason. The very
objects she sat on were considered unclean and could transfer her
uncleanness to anyone who touched them. Of course this followed
her into the kitchen, and any food she prepared would be considered
unclean. In other words, the woman with the issue of blood had no

life. She lived in isolation. Her disease and her unrelenting quest for a cure had cost her everything.

Finally, her faith propelled her. Her longing to be made whole and her belief that Jesus could make that happen superseded all else. She had been defined by her illness for far too long. In deep pain, weak, and humiliated, this precious woman squeezed and pushed her way past multitudes of people who crowded around Jesus on a dusty road. All of them wanted Jesus's touch.

But this woman dared to believe.

She strained, determined arms reaching out toward Jesus. Crawling behind Him, she looked up, her faith stretched, and she touched Him in a way no one else did.

And Jesus noticed.

When was the last time it cost us to reach out to Jesus? When was the last time we rose early to have time with Him, skipped our favorite book or TV show because we needed Him, or extended our prayer time because we were desperate enough to forgo all else? When was the last time we pushed past our pain, past our insecurities, past our uncertainties and, with believing hearts, reached out to the One who is approachable and available and in our very midst?

Jesus not only felt this woman's touch—her faith in action—He rewarded it. He searched the crowd, looking into the eyes of the one whose touch differed vastly from all those around Him. Though her illness lasted longer than she ever imagined, her healing took place in an instant. And Jesus spoke the words her heart longed to hear.

> He said unto her, Daughter, thy faith hath made thee whole;
> go in peace, and be whole of thy plague (Mark 5:34 KJV).

When we determine to push past all that entangles us, when we reach out to Him in spite of the cost, we will possess something priceless—a personal encounter with Jesus. And *that* is when wholeness begins.

Jesus healed countless people in Scripture. He made people whole then, and He makes people whole now. He is well able to heal our emotions, to remove the sting from bitter memories that make us ache inside. He is well able to heal our hearts and our bodies and transform our lives into something more beautiful than we ever imagined.

> Now to Him Who, by (in consequence of) the [action of His] power that is at work within us, is able to [carry out His purpose and] do superabundantly, far over and above all that we [dare] ask or think [infinitely beyond our highest prayers, desires, thoughts, hopes, or dreams]—To Him be glory in the church and in Christ Jesus throughout all generations forever and ever. Amen (so be it) (Ephesians 3:20-21 AMPC).

Our journey toward wholeness begins with daring to believe God. But there is so much more. We must ask God to show us how He sees us, to allow us to glimpse our potential instead of believing the worst of ourselves. Then we need to pray that we won't grow weary along the way, that we will cooperate with His Spirit, and that we can willingly relinquish our expectations concerning timing and how things should unfold. Finally, we must pray that our belief will propel us toward Jesus, the Author and Finisher of our faith.

I have not yet arrived. I'm not yet that radiant woman that God allowed me to glimpse many years ago. But I can't help but believe I'm eking closer. On some days, my hot mess of a self makes a staggering, embarrassing appearance. And on good days, His grace shines through, and my heart is penitently humbled and exceedingly grateful. Though parts of me are indeed still a hot mess, I am *His* hot mess. I'm on that narrow road to freedom, and I'm going to keep moving forward with Him as, little by little, He fulfills His beautiful promise to make me whole. A promise that will be made gloriously complete on resurrection morning.

Your Personal Proclamation:
SAY IT. KNOW IT. BELIEVE IT.

The One who created me sees my potential, and I have every intention of embracing it and living up to it by His grace. God's plans and power far exceed my flaws, my inabilities, and my past. He is taking all the fragments of my broken heart and broken life and making them whole. I will not try to make it happen but will rest in God's timing, nonetheless cooperating with Him as He reveals my part to me. I will not be ashamed of my scars, as they point to a mighty Savior, and I know that I overcome by the blood of the Lamb and the word of my testimony. I will choose to see through eyes of faith and believe that God is indeed at work, making me whole, and healing every soul fracture. The sweet breeze of freedom is blowing across my heart even now, and with everything within me I commit to cooperating with all of the Holy Spirit's work, trusting the Lord and moving forward into wholeness.

2

Wait! You Mean That's Not Who I Really Am?

I WILL GIVE YOU A NEW IDENTITY

*We are made right with God by placing our faith in Jesus Christ.
And this is true for everyone who believes, no matter who we are.*

ROMANS 3:22

Maybe it was the black tights gripping my head, waistband pressing into my forehead, stretchy legs cut and braided to resemble Indian ponytails. Maybe it was the oversized sweatshirt I wore as a fluffy, fake Indian dress. Or maybe it was the way all the kids stared at me, smirked, then whispered to each other before dissolving into fits of giggles. But before lunchtime on that Halloween day, this kindergarten student was calling home sick with a gargantuan stomachache.

Clearly, my mom's dubious, makeshift Halloween outfit was a bust.

When I shared this story with my then nineteen-year-old daughter, Emily, in her pragmatic way she replied, "You could've just taken the tights off your head, you know."

I laughed, but I didn't remove those tights. Highly compliant and fearful of my parents, I rarely did anything without permission. In spite of the awkward humiliation I felt even as I walked to school in the dreadful fake Indian outfit (kids on the other side of the street gawked in alarm), I left the costume firmly in place.

I was not scarred for life by the incident, but now I look back and wince just a little and wonder…why *didn't* I just take the tights off my head?

Be Careful What You Believe

The truth is simple. The beginning of some erroneous and fearful thought processes worked against me until I knew better: I did what I was told. I believed what others said. I accepted what people said about me.

Because my childhood home was mostly void of kind, encouraging, or even informative words, I absorbed what was readily available: ugly words, angry words, tense words. Defensive, rude, demeaning words. I also did a lot of piecemeal assuming, which meant I often felt liable for things beyond my control or responsibility. My little mind and heart were like so much inner Play-Doh, molded by whatever comments, words, or attitudes surrounded me. As Proverbs 23:7 tells us, "As he thinks in his heart, so is he" (AMPC).

Unfortunately, lots of people said many things to and about me, and my young heart unconsciously allowed their words and comments (true or not) to shape me. Actually, I assumed words spoken to me were true. And as I thought, so I was.

Can you relate to any of the following?

I did what I was told. I'm a rule-follower by nature. Just tell me what you expect, and I'm your girl. I have always respected authority, paid attention to instructions, and done my best to do my part. The only problem with all this is before I knew Christ and before I had His wisdom and His Spirit, I was told to do foolish things. Unwise things. Harmful things. Friends, acquaintances, rogue school teachers, and even my mom made ungodly suggestions to me which I sometimes willingly jumped into, and other times did against my better judgment.

I surmised the worst from silence and believed unspoken things. As a rule, my dad didn't engage in a meaningful way with any of us kids. On Friday mornings during the summer, I regularly accompanied him on the one-hour commute to Detroit, where he worked. He'd drop me off at my gram's house, where I'd stay for the weekend. On these drives, he never said a word to me. We rode in complete silence for 60 miles, and somehow his lack of words communicated plenty. I believed that I didn't matter; that I was clearly not worth talking to, not worth the effort, not valued. It makes sense that a young girl with the gift of communication—words—who desperately longed for conversation with her dad, would feel invisible and unworthy.

I accepted what others said about me. At the age of nine, I wrote my first book—a mystery, complete with a colored, stapled cover. Twenty-eight pages long, it told the story of young friends exploring an old, abandoned farmhouse, and what they discovered. Jubilant, I jotted in the final sentence, raced out to the family room, and handed it to a relative who was living with us at the time, then waited in my room for the response. Eager to hear what I hoped would be accolades, I was crushed instead to hear laughter. I hadn't written a single funny line in the entire story. Soon my relative brought my little story back to me, wiping his eyes as he continued to laugh. "You misspelled this word. Instead of *horrible*, it says *horrable*." He pronounced it *hor-abble,* over and over, laughing the entire time, and my heart absolutely sank. The torment seemed to go on for hours, every chuckle crushing me.

In spite of my love for writing, I started to understand that I was a horrible writer. I couldn't even spell, for Pete's sake. Humiliated and discouraged, I seriously doubted my abilities. What was the use?

Distorted by Shame

When I was about 11, two friends stepped inside our front door for the first time and gasped. Silent and wide-eyed, they stood scanning the rooms. Finally, one of them declared, "We've never seen a house like *this* before!"

I cringed.

Uneasiness waltzed right up my backbone, making me shiver. Accustomed to the filth and chaos that had surrounded me for as long as I could remember, I hadn't noticed the conditions around me. With new eyes, I took in my friends' view from inside our front door. Suddenly, my cheeks felt hot. Our living room, void of furniture, showcased multiple piles of dried-up dog filth, embarrassing monuments of neglect. Assorted dirty clothing, trash, empty cups, and encrusted dishes covered every surface. My home was, in a word, deplorable.

My four younger siblings ran around in mismatched, ill-fitting clothes, their hair tangled and dirty. The truth was, I didn't even know where to find a hairbrush. Or sheets for the bottom bunk where I slept. Or half the time, toilet paper. What wasn't visible from that vantage point were the empty kitchen cupboards, pantry, and refrigerator. But I had visited my friends' homes and knew other kitchens held bounties of cereal and fruit and Danish pastries and lunch meat and milk.

Those excruciating moments steeped my heart in deep shame. Humiliation clung to me on the inside, and from that point on I felt less-than.

Fast-forward to young adulthood. I had matured physically but, not receiving guidance concerning emotional well-being, wisdom, or even normal life, I just sort of floundered. I lacked a spiritual plumb line, along with even the smallest ability to discern truth from error. Worse, I didn't know who I was, except in the negative sense. So I used what I had—a cute figure and a pretty face (or so I was told)—to garner attention and affection and make my way in the world. I fell into and out of relationships, not recognizing or paying attention to the steep cost on my heart and soul. I had no knowledge of boundaries and allowed things to happen to me that I did not like or want. Over and over.

I lacked an intrinsic sense of value, security, self-awareness, confidence, and acceptance.

I think many women can relate. As I've shared bits and pieces of my story over the years, I've experienced nods of recognition, heartfelt emails, and heartrending comments left on my blog posts. So many children, it seems, grew up experiencing the same lack of a healthy, stable, loving family life. Lack of kind, encouraging, or even informative words. And Satan not only recognizes this, he capitalizes on it.

Instead of growing up knowing who we are in Christ, too many women grow up believing and accepting complete falsehoods about themselves. We grow up feeling insecure, less-than, unloved, fearful, and worse, lacking the awareness of and knowledge of how to do anything about it. For a long time I didn't realize change was necessary because I was unaware there was a problem to begin with. Oh, my heart tried telling me, but because of years of pain, neglect, and trauma,

I had learned to live in survival mode and completely tuned out my heart.

But my heart issues manifested themselves anyway—in unrealistic expectations, foolish demands, Yosemite Sam-style anger, and crippling insecurity. I was a smoking-hot mess.

When I became a believer at the age of 29, I was in my second marriage and the mom of two children. My house stayed immaculate, I loved to bake, held down a good job, got along with my neighbors, and adored my children to pieces. But I still embraced a negative, critical, utterly inaccurate concept of myself.

God was about to start shattering every one of those misconceptions. But first I had to discover they existed.

We Need Defensive Thinking

We're taught to drive defensively (at least that's how I learned eons ago, way back in high school driver's ed), always remaining alert to the cars around us, gauging what is going on and what could happen. Yet we are not taught to *think* defensively. We aren't taught to be alert or pay attention to what we think, believe, or accept into our minds and hearts. So as I grew into adulthood, these faulty thought processes still operated with carte blanche. I unwittingly embraced a completely distorted self-perception, allowing the enemy's blatant lies to continue shaping me.

Those hideous black tights are symbolic of what we permit to stretch across our brains: the dark beliefs and the lies that cover our minds. We walk along feeling humiliated, less-than. That's what the devil counts on. He is delighted and amused when we let him trespass in our minds, which enables him to tether us to a negative place.

When we pray for wisdom and use Scripture and the good minds God has given us, we can begin to recognize—and replace—wrong beliefs.

Each of the beliefs listed on the preceding pages followed me into adulthood. My perspective and understanding was skewed and, by then, each belief deeply imbedded. It was just the way I was. Or so I thought.

As a child, *I did what I was told.* But instead of automatically capitulating to orders we don't agree with or have peace about, we can allow ourselves time to think, pray, and come to a wise conclusion. We *never* have to do anything contrary to God's Word or that goes against our consciences.

I surmised the worst from silence and believed unspoken things. We can believe the best, prevent ourselves from making unwise assumptions, and ask God to fill the silent void with His reassuring truth and encouragement.

I accepted what others said about me. But instead of allowing unkind, untrue, erroneous opinions to puncture and settle into our hearts, we can guard our hearts, weigh words, and refuse those that will bring inner harm, while dwelling on what God's Word declares about us. We don't have to accept everything as fact. We can acquire discernment, filter information, research firsthand, and arrive at prudent decisions.

That's why Scripture warns us to be on guard:

> Stay alert! Watch out for your great enemy, the devil. He prowls around like a roaring lion, looking for someone to devour (1 Peter 5:8).

If the enemy can get us to accept that we are less than God says we are, if he can get us to believe that we are unloved, not valuable, ugly, unimportant, inept, less-than, unable to change (and more), then he has done his job and done it well. As a child, I was easy prey for the enemy. But even after I reached adulthood, and then after I became a believer, I continued hearing and automatically accepting his foul, angry, demeaning words. I simply didn't recognize his modus operandi. Further, I didn't realize I could be aware of and protect myself by protecting my thoughts.

The good news in 1 Peter is we do not have to allow what has always happened to continue. We can be in charge of our thoughts instead of accommodating every rogue thought (whether our own or planted by the enemy). We can take the stinkin' tights off our heads. In fact, we should. We must.

Fluent in the Culture's Lingo, Not Fluent in Scripture

One of the primary ways to take off the tights is through absorbing Scripture. Not just casually reading it, skimming it, or halfheartedly understanding it, but by devouring it. Drinking it in like a parched triathlete downs cold Gatorade. Allowing our hearts to be immersed and marinated in God's holy, powerful, life-transforming Word so that it sinks deep into our very marrow.

This means allowing Scripture, which is living and active and sharper than any two-edged sword (see Hebrews 4:12), to move and live and be active *in us*. As we become familiar with and absorb God's Word, a holy transformation begins—one that enables us to not only understand God's character, but enables us to begin to grasp the truth of who we really are.

> Don't copy the behavior and customs of this world, but let God transform you into a new person by changing the way you think. Then you will learn to know God's will for you, which is good and pleasing and perfect (Romans 12:2).

We learn to know God's will as we continue to absorb His Word and make time in our days for regular, intimate worship and prayer. As I began to mature in the things of God, my eyes were opened, and I recognized the need to be able to discern truth from error. To my surprise, I discovered that there is a Spirit of truth and a spirit of error (1 John 4:6). And I started to understand that I had embraced the spirit of error for most of my life.

It felt weird, as initially I was completely unaware that embracing a spirit of error had played such a huge part in my life. But by God's grace my awareness increased, and discerning truth from error became less confusing. It was sort of like putting on prescription glasses for the first time and feeling shocked at the clarity. The truth had been there the whole time, but I didn't have the eyes to see it. I began to understand some of the falsehoods that had molded and shaped me. I began to sense my intense need for healing and freedom.

Unfortunately, some of these inaccuracies had become deeply

embedded in my heart. There were days it seemed pointless to even try escaping them. Though my efforts were sincere, round and round I went, sensing I seriously needed to change but unable to make that authentic change happen. I desperately needed help.

Removing Embedded Restraints

I spotted the beautiful black Labrador retriever as I pulled my car into my veterinarian's parking lot. Roaming free and with no apparent owner in sight, I leashed my dog, Sophie, and we headed inside. Curious, I asked the receptionist about the loose dog. "Oh, that's Patty, Dr. G's dog," he said, as he pushed the door open and called Patty back inside the office.

The two dogs sniffed each other. "Well, she's adorable," I said, reining in my Australian shepherd.

"Actually, it's a he," the receptionist corrected me. But then the kennel attendant appeared, and it was time for me to escort Sophie back to her temporary living quarters.

After getting my dog situated, I walked back toward the front office, wondering why on earth my vet would name a male dog Patty. So before I headed out the door, I asked.

"Actually, his name is Padi, P-A-D-I, not Patty. He's a rescue. Someone discovered him chained and padlocked to a tree. When he arrived here, he was severely neglected; the chain and padlock had been around his neck for so long that it had literally grown into his neck. Dr. G. surgically removed the embedded padlock. Destroyed his voice box, but other than that, he's a great dog."

I tried to swallow, but my throat felt suddenly dry. Glancing down at Padi, my hand grazed the top of his head. "Good boy, buddy." A pink tongue hung out the side of his mouth, and his tail wagged. What a sweet, adorable dog. Friendly as could be.

Many of us are not only tethered to parts of our past, but the lies and distortions we've accepted for entirely too long have become deeply embedded in our souls. Though we attempt to do our part and sincerely love and trust the Lord, in those certain areas it feels like we are completely chained.

Satan's intentions are clear. The enemy wants to silence our voices and destroy our hope in believing that God's promises are actually true and actually for us. He wants to prevent us from discovering a balanced, biblical, healthy perception of who we are. He wants to inflict deep wounds that stop our praise and discourage us. He wants us wounded, confused, and angry at God. He wants to steal our destinies and kill any hope that we can truly change. He wants us so tightly chained we cannot move forward.

I looked into Padi's eyes, and sheer outrage banged against my heart. I'm certain God is far more outraged when, through our acceptance of the enemy's harmful deceptions, we end up shackled to outright lies, distorted truths, and misconceptions for so long they literally become embedded in our souls. They become part of who we are.

But God does not desire for us to be chained to fallacies. He wants us anchored in truth. As Jesus said to His followers:

> The Spirit of the LORD is upon me, for he has anointed me to bring Good News to the poor. He has sent me to proclaim that captives will be released, that the blind will see, that the oppressed will be set free, and that the time of the LORD's favor has come (LUKE 4:18-19).

Jesus is the chain breaker. And our time of His favor—our time of fresh, new freedom from every falsehood that has been embedded in our hearts and souls—has come.

And the beautiful part is, we don't have to be ashamed at where we are, but rather amazed at what Jesus offers: the chance to receive and be changed by His great love and limitless power.

Jesus so tenderly loves us. One of the most beautiful examples of Jesus's life-transforming love involves a woman who had been caught in the very act of adultery. Unfairly brought before Jesus without the man with whom she was accused, Jesus stood up to her accusers, most likely incriminating them by writing their names and their own dalliances in the dirt. He put the woman's accusers, who slunk away one by one, in their place, freeing her from the penalty of death, before telling her to go and sin no more (John 8:3-11). Can you imagine her initial horror and her humiliation turning into the stunning realization that she would not die? That Jesus forgave her? That He allowed her to go free?

That is love in action.

He knows *all* we've done—the good, the bad, the ugly. Yet, He does not accuse us. He stands with us. The Lord is more than able to put the enemy in his place and to tenderly, gently forgive and heal.

Jesus has compassion. He doesn't demand perfection; He requests honesty. When we are willing to face the truth about ourselves, He meets us right there, without accusation, and He loves us. He truly wants us free.

When we understand all that Jesus offers us, how He sees our junk—our past, our mistakes, our distorted ideas of who we are, and our pain-filled hearts—and loves us anyway, we are on the way to understanding how deeply He values us. He is perfection on our behalf. This is the very beginning of embracing who He says we are.

> He knows all we've done—the good, the bad, the ugly. Yet He does not accuse us. He stands with us.

The natural result of this deep level of knowing the Lord and allowing ourselves to be known is not only our own freedom, but our ability to encourage and inspire others toward freedom. This is part of His grand design, the big picture, and it all starts with allowing ourselves to be real with Jesus.

Embracing the Process

Jesus is the One who frees us from every painfully embedded misconception, but it is hard work and an ongoing process through which we must do our part. Once we have this measure of understanding, it eases our journey because we realize that discovering and embracing who God says we are happens in ever-increasing increments as we commit to faithfully walking with Him.

One of the major obstacles to understanding who God says we truly are, and the first thing we must deal with, is our need for deep, authentic forgiveness. Embracing who God says we are means embracing forgiveness. The woman caught in adultery desperately needed forgiveness and discovered it through an astonishing encounter with a loving Messiah. Should we desire or seek any less? Jesus meets us at the very places our hearts are accused. He longs to engage our hearts, and He offers complete forgiveness for every single sin.

Every white lie.

Every angry word.

Every haughty look.

Every broken promise.

Every lustful glance.

Every dropped opportunity.

Every wrong thought.

Christ's perfect atonement is available to each of us. We only have to accept it, understanding that when He uttered the words "It is finished" (John 19:30), He meant them. And His forgiveness is something we need to ask for and accept daily or hourly—or on *those* days, minute by minute.

I cling to this verse, which I urge you to commit to memory:

> If we confess our sins to him, he is faithful and just to forgive us our sins and to cleanse us from all wickedness (1 John 1:9).

But then we must take it a step further.

We must forgive *ourselves*.

I know it might seem almost ridiculous. But we can't move forward if we have a grudge against ourselves, if we're constantly berating ourselves over past foolish choices, bad decisions, and outright willing sin. Sometimes forgiving our own selves is the hardest thing to do. We look back and think, "If only I hadn't____." Hindsight provides fluorescent-light clarity by which we clearly see what we dearly wish we had cared about before. Acute regret meets us in the middle of the night, replaying scenes and choices we'd rather not remember. It chains us to the bad places we wish we could forget.

But forgiving ourselves and truly letting go of our past—whether it's ten years ago or ten minutes ago (hello?)—is not optional. Do we not think that the woman caught in adultery had to forgive herself? I've forgiven myself over and over because—you guessed it—I'm human. I fail, fall so short, and disappoint myself.

Forgiving ourselves is mandatory.

When we forgive ourselves, we are freed from the condemnation and guilt (and all sorts of other garbage) that chain us to the very place the enemy wants us to remain: the place of defeat. The place where we believe we can never change, and the place where we cannot even imagine, let alone embrace, God's promises and who He says we are. Accepting the forgiveness Christ offers and then daring to forgive ourselves breaks these embedded chains.

Go ahead and do it. Say out loud that you forgive yourself. If you're the journaling type, write it down (in ink!) and date it, so that the next time you feel condemned and chained to your past, you can remember that Jesus took it so it's gone, and you are clean. You are blessed because your sin is covered (Psalm 32:1).

The next step in the process of learning to believe God's promises and embrace who God says we are is learning to walk in the Spirit, not in the flesh.

The Spirit and flesh oppose each other and are constantly at war; that's what it will sometimes feel like as we begin walking in the truth of who God says we are: all-out war. Old, deeply embedded habits are hard (but not impossible!) to break, and the enemy doesn't want us progressing. Frankly, sometimes our own flesh holds us back. It wants comfort, and change is not always comfortable. It wants sameness. Not to be challenged. But the more we practice walking in the Spirit, the easier it becomes. It's sort of like a holy training process. As we make the ongoing decision to regularly walk in the Spirit, being led by and obedient to His promptings, progress begins to happen. And every step toward the beautiful truth God declares over us is a big step away from Satan's lies.

> Walk and live [habitually] in the [Holy] Spirit [responsive
> to and controlled and guided by the Spirit]; then you will
> certainly not gratify the cravings and desires of the flesh (of

human nature without God). For the desires of the flesh
are opposed to the [Holy] Spirit, and the [desires of the]
Spirit are opposed to the flesh (godless human nature); for
these are antagonistic to each other [continually withstand-
ing and in conflict with each other], so that you are not free
but are prevented from doing what you desire to do (Galatians 5:16-17 AMPC).

Living habitually in the Holy Spirit means we've created a new
plumb line; it's our goal, our reality, our normal. When we are controlled by, guided by, and responsive to the Holy Spirit, we won't give
in to our flesh or fall for and give place to the enemy's lies, and we will
no longer accommodate the distortions we've lived with for entirely
too long. This is where we begin to make serious progress.

Discovering Who We Really Are

I ran across the dirt road. "Hi! My name is Julie Kay Ett" I waved
to the lovely, brown-haired woman who smelled like flowery perfume.
For some reason, my eight-year-old self couldn't quite keep my name
straight.

My new neighbor, a sweet young mom with a blonde one-year-old
balanced on her hip, smiled, but her head tilted. "And I'm Lorie," she
said. "Nice to meet you." She retrieved her mail, while no doubt trying to figure out what strange kind of name the kid in her new neighborhood had.

But my name was not Julie Kay Ett. I'd gotten it turned all around
and basically said it backwards. My real name—the one that appeared
on my birth certificate—was Juliett Kay. I just didn't know it then.

I think that's how it is for so many of us. We unknowingly get
things turned around. Even after becoming believers and surrendering
our hearts and lives to Jesus, instead of knowing who we are in Him,
we adhere to names the Lord never intended for us: Insecure, Unloved,
Unknown, Fearful, Doubtful, Guilty, Depressed, Anxious—the list of
inaccurate, untrue names goes on. But God has stamped us with the
seal of His Holy Spirit. And that changes everything.

> In Him you also who have heard the Word of Truth, the glad tidings (Gospel) of your salvation, and have believed in and adhered to and relied on Him, were stamped with the seal of the long-promised Holy Spirit (Ephesians 1:13 AMPC).

We are His. We are not the sum total of all the awful things we've done or the hurtful things we've endured. Our true identities are eternally secure and sealed. Because of the finished work of the cross, God has stamped our hearts with His Spirit. We are approved and protected.

Not only that, but the Lord bestows on us fresh, clean, beautiful identities, and along with that, a new name: His beloved.

God wants us to know that...

- We belong to Him, and He belongs to us. "I am my lover's, and my lover is mine. He browses among the lilies" (Song of Songs 6:3).

- He loves us and has chosen us. "God loves you and has chosen you to be his own people" (1 Thessalonians 1:4).

- He has given us new names—new identities. "To everyone who is victorious I will give some of the manna that has been hidden away in heaven. And I will give to each one a white stone, and on the stone will be engraved a new name that no one understands except the one who receives it" (Revelation 2:17).

- In Christ, we are new creatures. "Anyone who belongs to Christ has become a new person. The old life is gone; a new life has begun!" (2 Corinthians 5:17).

- We can let go of our pasts—our regrets, our disappointments, our old ways of thinking, and anything else that holds us back. God declares fresh, new things over our lives. "Behold, the former things have come to pass, and new things I now declare; before they spring forth I tell you of them" (Isaiah 42:9 AMPC).

- It's a fight—something we have to willingly pursue, stand on, and hold on to. "Pursue righteousness and a godly life, along with faith, love, perseverance, and gentleness. Fight the good fight for the true faith. Hold tightly to the eternal life to which God has called you" (1 Timothy 6:11-12).

Not long ago I visited the Department of Motor Vehicles to update my driver's license. Like most states, Florida recently changed the identification requirements to comply with the new Department of Homeland Security enhanced driver's license protocol, causing no end of stress for drivers everywhere. Stories appeared in the local newspaper noting the stringent new requirements, along with the incredulous faces of some folks who, unaware of the new procedures, were unable to obtain an updated license. Even an 80-year-old woman with a perfect driving record who had lived in the same home for years had to produce further proof she was who her old license declared.

The entire state was in a tizzy. Those without passports were at a distinct disadvantage, and every citizen was placed in the position of having to prove they were who they said they were. Unhappy people were forced to dig out old birth certificates or locate their original marriage licenses—all to update the same driver's license they'd had for years. All this to prove your identity to a stranger behind a government desk who held the power to put the brakes on your license renewal.

Armed with that knowledge, I brought along my passport, original social security card, and an electric bill and hoped that would be enough. It wasn't. Thankfully, the DMV employee assisting me was kind-natured and asked if I had driven myself to their office. She then told me to fetch my vehicle title, and that would serve as the required final form of identification.

Finally, with great relief I stepped out of the DMV holding my new, updated, enhanced driver's license. I could now sail through airport security with ease, because all of my pertinent information was encoded and included.

Our inner identities are far more complex, of course, and so much more important. The Lord deeply desires to enhance our awareness of who He says we are. He longs for our hearts to be unchained, and for every rogue, untrue thought to be permanently abolished and replaced by His life-giving, empowering, sustaining, truth: that we are precious in His sight, that we are honored, and that He loves us (Isaiah 43:4).

My prayer is that as we explore God's promises together we will come away with a deeper, clearer, more accurate perception of our identities and God's awesome, far-reaching power and ability to heal and transform us. That we will shed the false and embrace the truth.

> We are His. We are not the sum total of all the awful things we've done or the hurtful things we've endured.

That the real *us* God intended—our healthy, radiant, beautiful, true selves—will emerge from beneath all of the encrusted lies and confusion and insecurities that have wreaked inner havoc and held us back from all God intends.

And that, by His great grace, we will arise with a new, enhanced, biblically accurate view of who we truly are. That we can walk through life with authentic dignity and holy ease, valuing ourselves because we know—we really know—that we are precious in His sight. That because He is faithful and more than able, even when we are a hot mess we can embrace our true identities and His stunning promises.

Your Personal Proclamation:
SAY IT. KNOW IT. BELIEVE IT.

I will think defensively: I will be careful what I believe about myself and pay attention to my thoughts, embracing God's truth and resisting the enemy's lies. I will resist the spirit of error and embrace the spirit of truth. I will allow Scripture, which is living and active, to live and be active in *me*.

Jesus has released me from my past; every embedded falsehood is broken off of me in His mighty name. I forgive myself for every foolish, wrong, sinful choice. My heart is unchained, healed, and renewed, and I am forgiven, accepted, and deeply loved by Him. By His grace I will arise with a fresh, new, biblically accurate view of myself. I will pursue and embrace God's promises. I will walk through life with authentic dignity and holy ease, and I will value myself because I am precious in His sight.

3

The Part Where We Keep Going Through Hard Stuff

I WILL WORK ALL THINGS FOR GOOD

But you must continue to believe this truth and stand firmly in it.

Colossians 1:23

It was the first and only time I read a Bible verse and instantly hated it.

I know. You're thinking we shouldn't hate Scripture—and I agree with you. But eons ago when I was a new Christian, I didn't realize you probably shouldn't loathe the Word of God.

So when a far-less-mature me stumbled across a particular verse in my Bible, a sandstorm of agitation, stinging and uncomfortable, pelted my heart. And I thought, *You've got to be kidding.* Allow me to introduce you to the infamous verse:

> Fear not [there is nothing to fear], for I am with you; do not look around you in terror and be dismayed, for I am your God. I will strengthen and harden you to difficulties, yes, I will help you; yes, I will hold you up and retain you with My [victorious] right hand of rightness and justice (Isaiah 41:10 AMPC).

Perhaps for you Isaiah 41:10 is a good verse, one that inspires courage. After all, God declares He will strengthen us and help us and even hold us up. And Lord knows I needed (and still need) holding up. A lot. Forever and always.

But at the time, that's not the part of the verse I focused on. Plagued by deep inner pain from a childhood marked by trauma, I felt overwhelmed at the thought of more suffering, which is how this verse filtered into my brain. Compounded by the excruciating difficulty and disappointment of my marriage, I was in no mood to read about being hardened to difficulties. To me, that verse shouted one thing—and it was the one thing I couldn't bear to hear: *Things are going to get worse. Much, much worse. But the good part is, you'll become as tough as the calluses on a ballerina's feet, and even though it'll be really, really hard, you'll be able to dance even when the ground gouges your feet because I will help you.*

The problem was, I didn't want to be tough. I couldn't imagine my sanity level if things spiraled. And I hated calluses. I always wore shoes—or at least socks. My feet (and heart) were delicate. Tender. Sensitive. And I liked them that way.

Hardship 101

This verse spoke of storms and heartaches and more hard circumstances that I didn't want to think about, much less endure. I didn't care if God said He would be there. I'd already had more than enough. As far as I was concerned, I'd already paid my dues—entirely too many dues, frankly—and I wanted happy verses. Verses that promised me everything was going to be all right. Verses that assured me God was in control, He loved me, and most importantly, He would prove His love for me by excusing me from future pain.

Sort of like a gold-plated get-out-of-jail-free card, only specifically for future pain or trouble of any kind.

In my mind, that meant all the issues plaguing my home life and, more notably, my inner life—the constant tension of unresolved conflicts and the accompanying anger, hurt, and ever-building resentment taking up more and more space in my heart—would evaporate like a rare Florida frost in the early morning sun. Wasn't that how faith worked?

If faith was the substance of things hoped for, I certainly had it. I had hopes galore. But if you've ever lived with the challenge of holding on to hope when answers don't come, you'll understand the strain it creates in our hearts. Scripture says "hope deferred makes the heart sick" (Proverbs 13:12), and that's exactly how mine felt.

Flummoxed and even hurt, I just didn't get it. I wasn't seeing what I yearned for—not by a long shot. Why wouldn't God rescue me and spare me further misery? I knew my desires weren't wrong. Emotional health, stability, and a strong, loving marriage are legitimate desires. I was trying hard to cling to God and truly trust Him. But wasn't life more than never-ending waves of turmoil? What about my hopes, my goals, my dreams?

I can't help but wonder if Joseph felt the same way.

Joseph has always intrigued me because out of all of his brothers—and there were 11 other boys in the family—God chose to bestow dreams upon him (you can read his amazing story in its entirety in Genesis 37–48). The Lord entrusted to Joseph mysterious, thought-provoking, aspiration-stoking images in the night. Vivid, distinct dreams that alluded to his high-ranking future—much to his brothers' annoyance.

> One night Joseph had a dream, and when he told his brothers about it, they hated him more than ever. "Listen to this dream," he said. "We were out in the field, tying up bundles of grain. Suddenly my bundle stood up, and your bundles all gathered around and bowed low before mine!" His brothers responded, "So you think you will be our king, do you? Do you actually think you will reign over us?" And they hated him all the more because of his dreams and the way he talked about them (Genesis 37:5-8).

Undaunted by his siblings' hateful response, when Joseph later dreamed yet another dream, he didn't hold back in describing it.

> Soon Joseph had another dream, and again he told his brothers about it. "Listen, I have had another dream," he

said. "The sun, moon, and eleven stars bowed low before me!" (Genesis 37:9).

He hadn't exactly learned from the first time around, and he told not only his brothers but also his father, who wondered at the meaning of the dream, seemingly incredulous. By this time his brothers were just about fed up with Joseph and what they considered his inflated dreamscapes. But Jacob (Joseph's father) wondered what it all meant (Genesis 37:11).

Joseph has often been portrayed as a braggart, but that's not how I see him at all, in spite of his brothers' opinion. I think that when God places stunning dreams in our hearts, it's natural to want to share them with people close to us—especially our family. But our family doesn't always support our dreams. In fact, they may scoff at or interfere with the precious promises we hold in our hearts. God chose to place Joseph into a family who did not value his God-given dreams. I believe He allowed this to test Joseph's mettle and ultimately to strengthen him to difficulties (there's Isaiah 41:10 again!). And I believe God does the same with us.

Through various circumstances, sometimes including others' jealousy, the painful lack of family support, or straight-up hatred, God tests our hearts, our faith, and our determination. According to the inescapable Isaiah 41:10, clearly we will endure hardship. How much hardship will be commensurate with our callings, but none of us are immune.

Sometimes God Allows Life to Get Ugly

I've already told you how I wrote my first book at the age of nine. Three staples held together its 28 pages, which featured a hand-colored cover. In sixth grade I went on to earn straight A's in my creative writing class. I just knew I'd eventually write a book. But then family life went downhill, and my writing pen not only fell to the ground, it got buried. Completely.

At 15, when most girls struggle to keep up with homework and friends and fashion, I struggled to prepare meals and care for two of my younger siblings. Since my parents' divorce, my two siblings and I had moved with our mom to a new town (the other two siblings now lived with our dad) where our mom had rented a house, which also meant we were in new schools. Though I felt relief that there were no more knock-down, drag-outs between our parents, our new place was sparse on furniture, food, and our mom's presence.

So after a rough week, including two days with zero food available to fix for dinner, I decided I had no choice but to locate our mom and ask her to bring home some groceries. I gathered my courage, pulled out the Yellow Pages, and dialed the number of the local bar where she usually hung out.

After asking to speak with her, a weird shudder crept up my back when I heard the manager holler my mom's name. When she finally answered, I kept it brief and pleaded for food. The words she hissed in response were not what I hoped to hear. But an hour later, when I heard the sound of keys in our front door, I felt relieved and hopeful. Sure enough, a brown paper sack was nestled in my mom's arm. Food!

I jumped up to help with the groceries but saw fierce anger in my mom's eyes and froze.

"This," my mom said as she approached me, holding up a gallon of milk, "is for you." Relief and fear swirled around my heart, an odd fusion warning me that something wasn't right.

I reached out to take the milk jug at the very moment my mom launched it across the room. Precious white liquid exploded all over the vinyl dining room floor.

"And so are these!" She heaved the bag of groceries onto the floor, clearly incensed that she'd been called away from the night's activities. A can of corn rolled into the center of the cold, white puddle.

My younger sister and brother both began to cry. Trembling, I turned from the mess on the floor to my mother. "What are you *doing*?"

Her voice dropped to an eerie whisper. "How *dare* you call me while I'm out."

My heart felt like it might slice right out of my chest. I tried to breathe. "But Mom, we haven't had food in the house for two days. We're all hungry."

"Don't you dare call me Mom. Don't *ever* call me Mom again!"

My crying siblings, the mess on the floor, and her fiery words were too much. Hot tears leaked from my eyes. I didn't understand. I had no idea what was happening.

Things got even more bizarre.

My mom opened her purse, unzipped her wallet, and pulled out a crisp one-hundred-dollar bill. I gasped. Then she withdrew another. And another. She started counting them. Five. Five one-hundred-dollar bills. Right in front of me. Our refrigerator was empty, but she had $500? My brain was officially on tilt.

Confused and frightened, I tried to figure out where this was going. I could never have imagined.

"From now on," my mother announced, "you are no longer a member of this family."

My heart lurched. Nausea hit deep in my stomach.

To the tune of my siblings' frightened whimpers, my mother lifted her hand over her head and threw the $500 at me. The money swirled down to the floor in slow motion. She looked me in the eye. "You are now a boarder here, and you will pay rent every month."

With that, she turned and stormed out the front door.

After comforting my little brother and sister, I made a desperate phone call to a relative and boarded a flight the next day to a more stable environment. Within weeks, my mom was claimed an unfit mother by the courts. My two siblings moved in with my dad, and when I caught my breath a few days later, I was 800 miles from home— a hurting, hot mess, in shock, and wondering at the strange turn my life had taken.

What I didn't understand as a teenager (and frankly still wrestle with as an adult) is the unsettling fact that God allows us to endure painful and sometimes traumatic events which, in His unfathomable ways, He is able to use, and which ultimately prepare us for His specific calling on our lives.

Joseph also endured some serious family dysfunction. His father sent him to check on his brothers and bring back word to him on how they were doing. Joseph could hardly have imagined where that simple trip would lead him (Genesis 37:14).

His jealous, cruel brothers ganged up on him while they were all far from home and, after initially dropping him into a dry well to die, changed their minds about killing him outright and instead sold him as a slave to random traders passing by. Right when God had poured out amazing dreams of promise to Joseph, it all appeared to come to a screeching halt. Joseph was deeply traumatized—snatched away from all he knew. Far from home, in his sorrow and grief he must have thought his dreams were as good as dead.

Why was God allowing such unbearable heartache?

For many excruciating years, Joseph suffered intense anguish that could only come by the betrayal of those closest to him. He faced the harsh sorrow of losing his beloved father—the dad who loved his son so deeply that he crafted a splendid, vibrant coat as an expression of his love for him (see Genesis 37:3). Then he was forced to leave his boyhood home, his homeland, and all he knew, coupled with the ache and injustice of slavery, and there was nothing he could do about it except hope and pray. Joseph spiraled from dreams of promise to becoming the property of someone else in a foreign land. He was owned by another.

When It Feels Like Our Circumstances Own Us

When our lives take a sharp turn in a direction we didn't see coming, when our God-given hopes and dreams are interrupted by forces over which we have no control, when it appears that our dreams have come to a heartrending end, it can feel like our circumstances own us. Like we are the helpless victims of a tragic scene that just keeps rolling the wrong way.

Like we've been taken captive, and there is nothing we can do.

But that is a lie.

The enemy wants us to feel defeated, deeply discouraged, and hopeless. But even when it feels like our circumstances own us, there are specific things we can do.

First, we can remember that God is sovereign, and that ultimately every season of our lives is in His hands. As the psalmist says, "My times are in Your hands; deliver me from the hands of my foes and those who pursue me and persecute me" (Psalm 31:15 AMPC). When we dare to believe (and keep believing!), we can be assured that, in the end, God's purposes always prevail.

Another thing we can do is pray. If the prayers of a righteous man are powerful and effective (And they are! See James 5:16.), then we can be sure that our prayers will move God and bring change one way or another. Scripture tells us to pray without ceasing (1 Thessalonians 5:17), to keep asking and it will be given to us (Matthew 7:7), and to pray at all times—on every occasion, in every season (Ephesians 6:18).

God uses our prayers. Our hands are never completely tied as long as we pray. And as Scripture says, He always listens, so we should always pray. You better believe I'm going to pray and keep praying. No. Matter. What. Psalm 116:2 assures us, "Because he bends down to listen, I will pray as long as I have breath!"

We can also ask God to gird our hearts and hold us in His supernatural peace—the mind-boggling peace that defies logic because it makes no sense, given the situation.

> Don't worry about anything; instead, pray about everything. Tell God what you need, and thank him for all he has done. Then you will experience God's peace, which exceeds anything we can understand. His peace will guard your hearts and minds as you live in Christ Jesus (Philippians 4:6-7).

Not only does His peace ease our souls, it shines bright and clear to those around us, inspiring encouragement and even divine curiosity. I think this is how Joseph lived. In the depth of his hurt, he asked God to help him, and God faithfully poured out His amazing, abundant peace. People around Joseph took notice of this peace—a supernatural peace the Egyptians were unaccustomed to seeing, particularly in a slave. Joseph turned out to be an incredible witness of his mighty God while living in a foreign land.

We can truly cast our cares on Christ. Just like a doting parent lifts their small child's heavy backpack and carries it for them from the bus stop, God stands next to us, arms extended, waiting for us to release the heavy things that weigh down our hearts. It's never God's desire for us to carry all the heavy junk that life throws our way. He is able. We are not.

And finally, we can trust that God is greater than the wretched, hard stuff. No situation has more control over us than God. He is always greater, far superior than any situation in which we find ourselves. When we remain near Him, keeping our hearts riveted onto Him and the truth of His Word, we are anchored in a safe, sweet place.

> He who dwells in the secret place of the Most High shall remain stable and fixed under the shadow of the Almighty [Whose power no foe can withstand] (Psalm 91:1 AMPC).

We can live in peace and stability when all hell is busting loose around us. We must simply choose to dwell with and near Him, never allowing our hearts to stray into the remote wilderness areas of fear and anxiety and discouragement.

But what about when things go from bad to worse? What about when things spiral unthinkably and get even more awful?

From Bad to *You've Got to Be Kidding*

I went from a rough childhood to launching out on my own at 17. I married for the first time at 18, divorced at 20, and raised my son as a single mom for five years. Then I met Keith. Though I sensed a distinct lack of peace about marrying him, I didn't yet know the Lord, nor did I understand that a lack of peace meant I shouldn't move forward. All I knew was I felt insecure, lonely, and afraid that no one would ever marry a single mom with crooked teeth. So we married.

And then things got really ugly. They truly went from bad to worse. My mess of a heart and mess of a marriage left me feeling imprisoned.

Unbelievably, things got worse for Joseph too. Joseph was handsome and well built, which Potiphar's wife clearly noticed (Potiphar had purchased Joseph). She repeatedly flung herself at Joseph, who did the right thing, nobly refusing her advances and making every effort to stay out of her way. He consistently acted uprightly and always refused her seductive advances (Genesis 39:7-10). Yet in an unimaginable blow of injustice, Potiphar's wife accused Joseph of attempted rape, and he landed in prison for a crime he would never dream of committing.

Joseph had no doubt begun to pull himself together after the devastation of being torn from his beloved home and his adored father. He had worked hard and gained the favor and esteem of Potiphar (see Genesis 39:4). But now he suffered a second massive, humiliating injustice. Already enslaved in a foreign land, he was now imprisoned, his heart crushed yet again.

Joseph was now literally in a prison within a prison.

There are times we're enduring a rough patch, and then something even worse happens. Why does God sometimes allow such intense waves of ever-increasing suffering into our lives? And is such suffering something we must endure...or can we escape it?

Scripture shows us that suffering is actually inseparable from Christianity, and that God Himself regards us favorably when we put up with or endure suffering. The apostle Peter wrote, "One is regarded favorably (is approved, acceptable, and thankworthy) if, as in the sight of God, he endures the pain of unjust suffering" (1 Peter 2:19 AMPC).

Peter is basically telling us that life won't always be fair. This is a hard truth to accept. But as Jesus said to His disciples, "If any of you wants to be my follower, you must give up your own way, take up your cross, and follow me" (Matthew 16:24).

I think we all have an innate sense of fairness and justice within us that automatically screams (mine screams at full volume) when something unfair happens. When my kids were young, they always extremely quickly pointed out when something wasn't fair. But Jesus enduring the cross because of our sin was not fair either. Hardships are something every believer must endure. The apostle Paul and Barnabas strengthened the believers in Lystra, Iconium, Antioch, and Pisidia by telling them things would not always be easy, "reminding them that we must suffer many hardships to enter the Kingdom of God" (Acts 14:22).

What I would like to know is, *How many, exactly?* Because *many* hardships and tribulations for *me* would be, oh, say three. Three is a good number. Yet, Paul considers suffering to be a special privilege we've been granted: "You have been given not only the privilege of trusting in Christ but also the privilege of suffering for him" (Philippians 1:29).

I know. It's shocking. The American dream of a life of ease doesn't exactly line up with Scripture. Apparently, there's just no way around the fact that not one of us is guaranteed an earthly life without suffering in one form or another. But why would God allow us to suffer? Doesn't He want us to be happy?

The surprising answer is that suffering is an awfully good teacher. "My suffering was good for me," said the psalmist, "for it taught me to pay attention to your decrees" (Psalm 119:71).

Our suffering is not for nothing—the Lord uses it. Every last bit. Every hurt, every injustice. It not only teaches us; it makes us more like Him. We are probably never more like Jesus than when we are suffering. And if we continue to trust and obey, even when it costs us, we will grow in godly character. If we're willing, we can allow our difficult circumstances to become teaching tools in God's hands.

Yes, Joseph was cruelly enslaved. Then he was wrongly imprisoned. Doubly imprisoned. And I can't help but wonder if Joseph wrestled with intense hopelessness. Don't we? When things go from bad to worse, aren't we tempted to throw in the towel, give up our hope, and call it a (very bad, awful, miserable, I've had it) day? (Or life?)

If and when God allows things to go from bad to worse in our lives, we would be wise to recognize that the enemy wants to use the whole from-bad-to-worse scenario to infuse hopelessness into our souls. We would be wise to understand that the enemy has a scheme. God's Word says we can do that, you know.

If through discernment we remain aware of Satan's schemes, then it shouldn't surprise us that he intends to cause intense pain. The enemy is ruthless. And his goal is to keep us focused on the pain long enough for seeds of resentment and bitterness to grow. The enemy wants us doubly imprisoned with no hope of escape.

Forgiveness Is Hard. Do It Anyway.

Our choices are clear: We can become enslaved to bitterness because of the injustice of our circumstances, situations, griefs, and disappointments, or we can choose to forgive and entrust our future and our very lives into God's hands.

Our pain is the result of sin. Our own sin and the sin of those close to us. And it pains me to admit that I wasted a lot of years imprisoned in bitterness and resentment. Though I had committed my life to the Lord, attended church regularly, and read my Bible like crazy (which helped significantly and was an undeniable, essential part of my healing process), I couldn't fathom forgiveness because it felt like letting the other person off the hook (wrong, wrong, wrong!). At the time, I did my best to cooperate with the Holy Spirit and with what I read in Scripture, but the deep wounds of my heart kept me imprisoned.

But God was faithfully at work. Little by little, He opened my eyes and helped me recognize my need to forgive. Truly forgive. Willingly forgive. As I cooperated with the Holy Spirit, I chose to forgive—over and over—letting go of my right to be right (that was a hard one!), my right to be angry, and my right to be resentful.

So, so not easy. So, so worth it.

As I have forgiven—over and over, and often through gritted teeth and void of the lovely feelings one would hope would accompany the offer of forgiveness but rarely does because, hello, forgiveness is hard (and in my experience is never, ever accompanied by soft background music)—I have become more and more free. Initially, it felt like an enormous price (I think forgiveness feels that way), but in the end I experienced the cleanness of God's forgiveness and the peace of releasing all my hurts, disappointments, and injustices to Him.

Forgiveness is God's way. And it's what He requires of us. Daily. Sometimes moment by moment. With all my heart, I want to follow His way, not my own.

In spite of the gut-wrenching circumstances he endured, there is no record of Joseph maintaining a bitter attitude. That does not mean he didn't struggle, but Joseph's circumstances didn't own him because he chose to forgive. Eventually, he reconciled with his brothers, revealing himself to them through anguished tears (see Genesis 45). This was possible because he had forgiven them long before they ever showed up in Egypt.

Fruitfulness in the Hard Spot

Sometimes God places us in difficult situations and, surprisingly, He then uses us to accomplish His will—while we're yet imprisoned. This totally blows my mind and thrills my heart all at once. In my super-organized, linear, logical manner of thinking, here's how it would go down: God would save us, *then* radically transform us, and *then*, when we're practically walking on water, He'd see we're ready and would use us to accomplish His plans and purposes.

Yet God's ways are not our ways (Isaiah 55:8-9). He lovingly sees our potential and pulls it out of us, and not always at what we might consider the most convenient or even appropriate of times.

After spending two years in Michigan, our family moved back home to Florida for my husband's new dream job, which he loved. I was homeschooling our two youngest kids (the oldest was already out of the house), and the Lord had opened the door immediately (or pushed me through it, depending on how you look at it…) for me to get involved in women's ministry at the church we had joined after we relocated to Florida.

One Tuesday morning our women's ministry hosted a guest speaker, who called me to the front of the meeting room to share a specific word God had given her for yours truly. I hardly could have anticipated what God was about to speak through her. With trepidation I walked up to the podium and waited.

Here's what I anticipated hearing: *You poor thing. Your marriage and heart are a wreck, and life is hard for you, so I'm going to supernaturally move and change it all. Now.*

Instead, here is what the guest speaker actually said: *I have deposited much in you, and it is time for you to start pouring out. I know it is hard, but unpack the boxes of your heart and pour out what I have placed within you.*

It made no sense to my brain. I was ready to leave a hard marriage and had no plans to use my gifts (whatever those were). I was flummoxed and struggled to understand how, and even why, God would use me when I was still experiencing so much heartache and my response to the whole mess was so raw and ugly.

Yet God is sovereign, and surprisingly, deep down my heart bore witness to the words spoken over me that day. Like with Joseph, the Lord uses all the hard, difficult things to prepare us. And just because He is still working *on* us doesn't mean He cannot work *through* us… even when it surprises us.

As we faithfully cooperate with the Lord through our hard stuff (over and over!), we discover that God doesn't just pull us out of the pit; He pulls the pit out of us. Clearly, pain and hard circumstances do not excuse us from the calling God has on our lives. He enables us to be fruitful not because of our anguish, but in spite of it.

In the midst of his captivity, God used Joseph. Mightily. The Lord's plans and purposes prevailed. And when we entrust our lives completely to Him, obey Him, and dare to believe in spite of how things appear, He does the same for us. Even when we've endured hardship for years. Even when circumstances hold us against our will.

The primary key to fruitfulness in the midst of our most distressing trials, our heartache, and our excruciating disappointment—our land of grief—is to know what Joseph knew.

> *But the Lord was with Joseph*, and he [though a slave] was a
> successful and prosperous man; and he was in the house of
> his master the Egyptian (Genesis 39:2 AMPC, italics mine).

Joseph knew God was with him, enabling him to prosper and be fruitful even in the midst of his intense grief and suffering. In fact, Joseph named his second son in honor of this fact: "Joseph named his second son Ephraim, for he said, 'God has made me fruitful in this land of my grief'" (Genesis 41:52).

Joseph recognized God's favor on his life, even while he lived in captivity.

What if God is a God of the journey—a God who mostly brings us into freedom in (often painfully slow) increments, all while choosing to use us right where we are?

If you think God would never ask a person to remain in difficult circumstances, think again. God isn't as interested in rescuing us out of our circumstances and relieving our pain as He is in allowing those circumstances to propel us more deeply into His arms, change us more into His image, and amazingly, use us precisely how He pleases.

Tough seasons give us the opportunity to grow in godly character. What makes us think we can become Christlike without suffering? Jesus was ridiculed, betrayed, rejected, and ultimately gave His life.

> Since we are his children, we are his heirs. In fact, together with Christ we are heirs of God's glory. But if we are to share his glory, we must also share his suffering (Romans 8:17).

Will we allow our hard circumstances to hinder us? Or will we instead let them shape us, train us, and propel us into God's presence while we continue holding on to holy hope? The kind of hope that is a concrete, stabilizing force in our hearts and lives because we trust that He is working all things for our good (Romans 8:28). The kind of hope that dares to believe that even if things don't go according to our plan, they will go according to His plan, which is even better. This holy hope upholds us and never "disappoints or deludes or shames us, for God's love has been poured out in our hearts through the Holy Spirit Who has been given to us" (Romans 5:5 AMPC).

Ultimately, the Lord allowed Joseph to be taken where he did not want to go, and though the same sometimes happens to us, it is always for a reason. When we keep going through hard stuff, over and over, it's not for nothing. Our circumstances—combined with God's plan—always, always hold divine purpose. We must believe that! If, like Joseph, we react nobly and pursue excellence, honoring God through it all, many will be touched, changed, even saved, because God intends it all for our good.

> God doesn't just pull us out of the pit; He pulls the pit out of us.

Every painful, awkward, embarrassing, gut-wrenching, tragic situation holds divine potential IF we will dare to believe God's truth and stand firm. He sees the big picture. He knows where all this is heading, and He loves us. And He truly works all things for our good.

Your Personal Proclamation:
SAY IT. KNOW IT. BELIEVE IT.

I will not shrink back from unpleasant, hard things God allows in my life because I dare to believe that God is sovereign and working all things for my good. He is enabling me to firmly hold on to faith and hope and making me fruitful in my land of heartache and grief.

I will not wish for a life of ease. I will allow the Lord to strengthen me and harden me to difficulties. I will face reality, my hand firmly gripping His. I will not allow myself to entertain defeat, discouragement, or hopelessness. When I am tempted to quit, I will run to the Lord and dwell in the secret place of the Most High. I will not be swayed by my circumstances or by fear. I will not give in or give up, but I will continue to stand firmly in God's truth.

4

The Chasm-Closer
I WILL ENABLE YOU

*"What do you mean, 'If I can?'" Jesus asked. "Anything
is possible if a person believes."*

MARK 9:23

Keith wooed me sweetly at the beginning of our relationship. He'd tie a small plastic grocery bag containing a box of my favorite Pepperidge Farm chocolate chip macadamia nut cookies to the front doorknob of my teeny one-bedroom apartment, knowing I would find them (and sigh) when I arrived home from work. But once we said, "I do," it didn't take long for things to spiral. Sweetness evaporated, replaced by negativity and critical anger. So the start of our marriage turned out to be not only rocky, but a full-out, slow-motion avalanche. Two deeply wounded, maladjusted people doing life together without Jesus is a scary scenario.

And those are probably the exact words I could use to describe the beginning of our marriage. Scary scenario.

Many years into our frozen snowslide in progress, I arrived home from church service one Sunday evening with our two young children and began fixing them a snack. My husband did not yet know the Lord, nor had Jesus had sufficient time to tame the *Stands with a Fist* portion of my heart (which was most of it). When Keith unleashed unkind words on me, my defiant heart retaliated, and the rumblings of a fresh avalanche ensued.

At some point, I sank into the loveseat in our family room and tuned out the harsh words. I was weary of the fight. Weary of defending myself. And weary of the tumultuous atmosphere of our home. Hot tears welled up in my eyes. Frankly, I didn't know how much longer I could go on …or even if I should. A massive chasm existed between what I longed for and the actuality of my married life.

A chasm is the gaping hole between God's promise and our reality. Many times the chasm we face is disappointment. Sometimes it's massive disappointment. A deep hurt. The stomach-churning letdown of a harsh reality we never saw coming.

Chasms are impossible to ignore because there's no denying the facts. When we stand on the brink of one, it seems to be taunting us. We could never bridge a chasm under our own power. And that is where I stood in my marriage: staring down into the abyss of a massive crater of hurt and disappointment I couldn't fathom maneuvering.

Though I sensed God leading me to remain in my marriage and assuring me He was at work behind the scenes, I nonetheless felt myself wobbling between believing Him and believing the ugly right in front of me. It's no doubt the reason Scripture admonishes us to walk in faith instead relying on what we see (2 Corinthians 5:7).

The circumstances before our eyes hold great sway over our hearts. And our hearts can either nurture or ruin our faith.

I think we all eventually end up in this very place. The place where we must face the ugly, massive chasm and decide whether or not we believe anyway. The place where we can choose to disregard what we see with our eyes and instead cling to what we perceive with our hearts. The place where we decide that either we're all in, or we not only throw in the towel, but stomp all over the blasted thing (and I have lived through some serious towel-stomping moments).

As I sensed the Holy Spirit compelling me to continue on in my marriage, indeed to continue on in all that I sensed Him calling me toward (though He had not yet revealed much of it to me), my heart longed to obey. So I stepped—one obedient, hesitant, cautious toe at a time. With every inch forward, I raised my eyes and my heart heavenward. *Are You sure, God? Are You really, really sure?* Because I sure wasn't. I wasn't sure at all.

And I think that's okay. Stepping forward in caution is better than not stepping forward at all. It is wise to move slowly, straining to sense holy confirmation, awaiting God's assurance as we trust that He knows what He is doing, even if we don't.

So when we find ourselves at the edge of a gaping chasm, wondering what on earth we're doing there, how do we know if or when to step forward? How can we advance when there's a massive hole? When there's a massive gulf between who we want to be—who God has called us to be—and who we are? Between where we want to be—in life, in ministry, our marriage, our career, all of our hopes and dreams—and where we actually are?

The most important thing we can do at the brink of a chasm is listen to the right voice.

The Enemy's Taunts

The fourteenth year of faithful King Hezekiah's reign over Judah was not a good one. King Sennacherib of Assyria came to attack his kingdom, took every ounce of gold and silver King Hezekiah offered him (it was tons, actually) to just go away, and then decided to attack anyway. What's worse, Sennacherib started it all with a massive propaganda campaign, sending his personal representative to bombard Hezekiah and his people with lies designed to undermine their very faith.

> The Assyrian king's chief of staff told them to give this message to Hezekiah: "This is what the great king of Assyria says: *What are you trusting in that makes you so confident?*" (2 Kings 18:19, italics mine).

Clearly, the king of Assyria noticed Hezekiah's confidence. Does the enemy see our confidence? Do others? Do they know what we are trusting in?

When the enemy's bombardments of our minds begin, do his malicious words ring true to us? Do we agree with him? Often the enemy's lies possess a measure of truth. Think about that. The enemy attempts to subtly bring us into agreement with him. He delights in pointing out what we know is true, even if it's not the entire truth. Even if it's a skewed truth. He capitalizes on our natural human tendencies toward doubt and awareness of our inadequacies, hoping to lure us into step with him. Why? The enemy wants to undermine our confidence in God's ability and faithfulness. And ultimately, he longs to do two things: diminish our faith and stop us from stepping forward.

On and on the taunts and accusations continued, hammering at the people's confidence on every level. The Assyrian king even had the audacity to insinuate that the Lord Himself could not rescue them from him, saying, "What makes you think that the LORD can rescue Jerusalem from me?" (2 Kings 18:35).

It's the enemy's scheme to sow seeds of doubt, confusion, and discouragement into our hearts so that we believe the chasm before us is far too wide. The relentless attack starts with a question: *What makes you think?* It's as if right when disappointment hits and the chasm is revealed, the enemy discovers our deepest fears and doubts, then attacks specifically in that area. His goal is to create a compelling statement that we not only resonate with but that we will agree with inwardly, so that our faith is undermined and weakened.

What makes you think?

What makes you think you can pursue that dream? What makes you think you can lose that weight? What makes you think you can apply for that position? What makes you think this miserable marriage is worth holding on to?

It's relentless.

And it was a relentless attack on the people of Israel. Yet their king had wisely forewarned them. Anticipating the king of Assyria's propaganda, King Hezekiah told his people not to answer the enemy's taunts (verse 36).

The people did not respond. They wisely heeded the advice given by their king. Do we? Are we yielded to the Holy Spirit, even when it means clamping our mouths closed? Do the enemy's taunts hit our forewarned hearts, so his truth-twisted words cannot possibly sink in?

Do we engage with the enemy, or do we engage with our God? Do we allow the enemy's taunts to shake us, or do we stand, chins high, eyes and heart locked on Jesus? Do we listen to the enemy? Or do we listen to the Lord over the clamor of our circumstances?

It's Christianity 101, but at times like these it is worth revisiting the simple, beautiful truth:

> [The flock] won't follow a stranger; they will run from him because they don't know his voice…My sheep listen to my voice; I know them, and they follow me (John 10:5,27).

It takes a sensitive heart in tune with the Holy Spirit to hear what God is saying when we teeter. If we are alert and wise, we will follow the Spirit's leading and know when to engage the enemy and when to remain silent. We will know when to respond and when to stand in faith. We will hear the Lord's voice over the enemy's propaganda.

A Chasm with a Purpose

Years ago when I was on the brink of my first national article appearing in a major publication, I quivered on the inside. I didn't understand how God could use me—a nobody from nowhere, who lacked formal training to boot. I truly wrestled with feeling utterly unqualified. Yet as I prayed about it, the Lord reassured my anxious heart. I sensed Him saying, *I taught David through fields of affliction, and I've taught you the same way.*

What if our current, disappointing chasm holds the potential to shape our character and train us? If God is truly sovereign, then everything in our lives serves a purpose. Even the chasms that present so much hardship and suffering. Because if we are willing, it is through these very things that we learn. Even Jesus and King David both learned this way.

King David wasn't born into royalty. He didn't just waltz over and decide to fight Goliath one day. He was trained. His preparation began as a young boy when he fought the lion and the bear as he watched over his father's sheep (1 Samuel 17:36). Armed with those experiences, he then faced down and slew Goliath while still a boy (1 Samuel 17:49). He allowed his circumstances to shape his character and train him. He didn't resent what some (like his brother, in verse 28) considered his lowly position, but was humbled and trained through it. David allowed his circumstances to refine him. He embraced where God placed him and worked hard at excelling and developing strong, godly moral character.

Once David was anointed as king, most scholars estimate it was 15 (or more) years before he actually became king. Who of us can imagine God revealing a divine purpose and then waiting, waiting, waiting, while we calmly, peacefully go about our regular old business until it actually happens—15 years later? (Wouldn't there be, at the very least, a conniption or two?) Yet, David did not pout or throw a fit or languish or waste his life.

He did his best to serve King Saul, who became wild-eyed jealous and sought to kill him. By necessity David then became a fugitive and lived in caves. What a far cry from the thrill of kingly anointing oil pouring over his head at the hand of the prophet Samuel (1 Samuel 16). For years a massive chasm existed between the promise that David was God's chosen king and the reality of running, running, running for his very life.

Yet David matured in the Lord, and he grew in grace and godly character. As the psalms that he penned show, the Lord used such times to transform, strengthen, and prepare David:

> O Lord, You have heard the desire and the longing of the humble and oppressed; You will prepare and strengthen and direct their hearts (Psalm 10:17 AMPC).

He uses such times to lead and teach us:

> Show me the right path, O LORD; point out the road for me to follow. Lead me by your truth and teach me, for you are the God who saves me. All day long I put my hope in you (Psalm 25:4-5).

He uses such times to counsel us:

> The LORD says, "I will guide you along the best pathway for your life. I will advise you and watch over you" (Psalm 32:8).

It turns out that God trained David through all he endured, and He does the same for us. During those seasons, David wrote many beloved psalms that still bring fresh encouragement thousands of years later (see Psalm 31, 57, and 59, to name a few). The priceless lessons he learned can transform our waiting at the edge of our chasm into a time of transformation if we are willing and as we grow to understand God's ways, which are high above our ways (Isaiah 55:9).

As we step forward obediently, it is always because God is working both in and through us, providing the desire, the energy, and the power to accomplish what He is leading us toward at any given moment. Even chasm-facing moments. Especially chasm-facing moments.

> [Not in your own strength] for it is God Who is all the while effectually at work in you [energizing and creating in you the power and desire], both to will and to work for His good pleasure and satisfaction and delight (Philippians 2:13 AMPC).

As we discover that our chasms hold divine purpose, we also learn that God Himself is there with us.

The Best Place to Be

What if we stop for just a moment and ask God for fresh perspective? What if our chasms—and yes, there will be more than one in our lives—are also opportunities for God to show Himself strong?

Could it be that even a massive chasm is no deterrent to the One who allowed it into our lives? Could it be that even our weak ineptness and our startling inadequacies can be turned to strength when our hearts are fully committed to Him?

Back to King Hezekiah and the king of Assyria, who was in full attack mode. His propaganda was spreading fast, and if you're anything like me, you understand how vulnerable a woman's emotions can be when we're hit over and over and over with the lies that hold a measure of truth and almost begin to make sense. This is when our chasms loom particularly large. The battle is starting, and we hardly know how to move forward.

King Hezekiah and his people were in a dilemma. Then in His perfect timing, God Himself steps in, accomplishing what they could not. Listen to what the Lord declares to Hezekiah through the prophet Isaiah:

> After King Hezekiah's officials delivered the king's message to Isaiah, the prophet replied, "Say to your master, 'This is what the LORD says: *Do not be disturbed* by this blasphemous speech against me from the Assyrian king's messengers. Listen! *I myself will move against him*, and the king will receive a message that he is needed at home. So he will return to his land, where I will have him killed with a sword'" (2 Kings 19:5-7, italics mine).

Do not be disturbed.

Yes, things aren't looking so great. Yes, fear is starting to shake us. Yes, the chasm is massive. But God is bigger. He is able. We must not allow the enemy's lies to disturb our hearts. We must learn not to surrender our peace, even when our feeble efforts are no match for the situation. Jesus reminded and urged us:

> Do not let your hearts be troubled, neither let them be afraid. [Stop allowing yourselves to be agitated and disturbed; and do not permit yourselves to be fearful and intimidated and cowardly and unsettled] (John 14:27 AMPC).

Does it occur to us that fear and agitation are optional? When we remain close to Jesus, our perception is far more accurate. We're more inclined from this near-to-Him vantage point to see things accurately. As the Prince of Peace fills us with His supernatural peace, we are far less likely to take the enemy's propaganda bait and far less likely to allow ourselves to be agitated and disturbed. It's always a choice.

But that's not all. God has more to say. And it's with intense relief we can absolutely inhale the following words from His heart to ours:

I myself will move against Him.

This is God's promise to us when our adversary hits us over and over with his twisted words. This is where our amazing heavenly Father steps in and deals with what we are ill-equipped to handle. This means we don't have to because God will. This means we can entrust the very thing that appears so impossible into His capable hands.

I myself will.

When we cannot, He will. We must let Him.

During the times I feel overwhelmed and uncertain, I can honestly say that my faith in God's ability never swerves. I know and firmly believe God can do anything. Anything. But I seriously doubt my *own* abilities to make it through, around, or over the obstacles.

It was at this particular time in my marriage and life in general when I was feeling particularly overwhelmed that God gave me a vivid dream:

I drove directly behind a supersized bulldozer on a bumpy, dusty, dirt road under major construction. On both sides of the road huge trucks worked: dump trucks, cement trucks, cranes, graders—you name it—along with dozens of working men wearing orange vests and hard hats.

Dirt and debris flew across my windshield as I closely trailed the bull-dozer. The uneven, angled road shifted from steep to narrow. Enormous holes made the drive treacherous.

It took every bit of energy and concentration I possessed just to remain behind the bulldozer. As long as I remained focused, my own vehicle was able to stay the course right behind it. I determined that no matter what, I would do whatever it took to stay close, safely behind the bulldozer lead-ing the way.

I awoke from that dream amazed and encouraged. God had given me a picture of not only what He was doing in my life, but what was required of me—and all of us—as we attempt to move forward while facing seemingly insurmountable obstacles.

God's part is to clear the way for us. He removes obstacles, accomplishing the heavy moving and lifting that we cannot manage.

> Do not be afraid or discouraged, for the LORD will person-ally go ahead of you. He will be with you; he will neither fail you nor abandon you (Deuteronomy 31:8).

Our God goes before us, and we must follow Him. It's our primary job description. As Jesus tells us, "If any of you wants to be my follower, you must give up your own way, take up your cross daily, and follow me" (Luke 9:23). We must also be determined. This is not a casual decision to see how things go. We must make the willing choice (daily, hourly, even second by second, if necessary) to do everything it takes to pursue God and keep moving forward—toward healing, wholeness, freedom, and spiritual maturity. Assume it won't be easy.

We must then remain actively close to God. This requires hard work. The Lord was moving fast, and it truly required all my effort not to fall behind. Sometimes life is crazy, but regardless of how fast it flies by, we need to do our part and make every endeavor to stay close to the Lord, in step with Him. We must guard our time with Him above all else, remain rooted in His Word and His presence, and pray without ceasing.

> What if our chasms—and yes, there will be more than one in our lives-are also opportunities for God to show Himself strong?

Finally, we must stay focused. All the activity on both sides of the road competed for my attention. Yet a glance in either direction would cost me. Isn't this a remarkable picture of our lives? Distractions abound (Hello? Facebook!), but those who are consistently focused on the Lord, who remain close to Him, will continue moving forward unimpeded.

Meanwhile, Back in Avalanche Land

Back to that unhappy Sunday evening in my family room and avalanche-ville. My weary heart was on the verge of quitting. I wasn't sure how much longer I could go on, or even if I should. Discouragement had me around the throat, choking out every last ounce of hope that things would ever change.

That's when I heard a gentle Voice speaking beautiful, hope-filled words so clearly I turned my head to see if someone stood behind me. With no angel in sight, those private, remarkable words nonetheless girded my heart in an amazing way, taking away my breath and my doubts.

God spoke fresh, perspective-changing truth to me that Sunday evening. He assured my weary heart that He saw the hurt and the disappointment, and that He was going to sovereignly accomplish what I could never in a million lifetimes manage. In the midst of my inability, God swooped in and assured me He was able.

I myself will.

He also spoke my name. It's what the Lord does. He speaks our name. He calls us out of our heartache and disappointment and looks into our eyes. Suddenly, our perspective shifts; our hopes are revived. It's what He did for Mary, who searched the empty tomb and, confused and weary, sat down in deep mourning and wept.

But the Messiah knew her and saw her and sought her out:

> "Mary!" Jesus said. She turned to him and cried out, "Rabboni!" (which is Hebrew for "Teacher") (John 20:16).

He knows us and knows what we're enduring. He seeks us. He speaks our name. He draws our attention away from the confusion and pain. And when we turn to Him, our hearts are always surprised and delighted and amazed. Oh Lord, give us ears to hear You when we tiptoe on the precipice of the chasms of disappointment and heartache. Give us ears that hear what You are speaking to us through Your Holy Spirit even now!

On a Sunday evening, Jesus suddenly appeared to His disciples. He spoke peace to them and breathed fresh life into their weary hearts. As John 20:22 records it, "He breathed on them and said, 'Receive the Holy Spirit.'"

The Maker of all life, the One through Whom all things live and move and have their being, the very One who breathed into Adam's nostrils, breathed on His disciples. And He breathes on us.

It's how He equips us. It's intimate. It's personal. It's real. He enables us and equips us through His breath of life. Through the power of the Holy Spirit. The last thing He said to His disciples that evening is what

He speaks to each one of us: "Don't be faithless any longer. Believe!" (John 20:27).

It's the deepest longing of my heart—that I won't be faithless, but believe.

As God spoke to me that Sunday evening many, many years ago, I sat incredulous at the warm promise delightfully spilling into every chamber of my heart in spite of our home's frigid atmosphere. Surprised by unfamiliar hope that night, I perceived that the God for Whom all things are possible was daring my overwhelmed heart to believe that change in my heart, my husband, and my marriage were not only possible, but imminent. I sensed Him beckoning me to a whole new level of faith, and I felt myself teetering on a precipice between the reality of the constant ache of a miserable marriage to an unbelieving husband, and the radiant promise making the hairs on the back of my neck tingle.

Initially, I couldn't figure out how on earth God would change my marriage. And though I felt confused and struggled to understand what, exactly, the Lord might mean, my heart nonetheless rejoiced. This holy promise glimmered with the hint of a potential transformation I'd hardly believed possible. And in spite of the unpleasant reality I currently faced, a white-hot spark of undeniable hope crackled into my heart.

Isn't that precisely what our hearts need when we face a massive chasm with no clue how to move forward and reach the other side? A spark of hope that ignites our hope and enables us to believe that God is greater. That He is higher. That He is able.

God is inviting us to step over the jagged fissure of hopelessness onto the even scarier ground of daring faith—an uneven, slippery place that will require all our concentration just to remain upright. So that's what I did. It was a place of uncertainty, but I didn't care. God had spoken to my heart, and I was compelled toward the very edge of all I believed.

This step of faith doesn't imply that we blindly deny facts. We cannot deny the facts. We must not. It would be most ludicrous, and denial is not what God requires. Faith is acknowledging and facing the facts but still believing the promise. It is holding on to the promise like we hold on to a passport when we visit a foreign country. Our passports prove who we are, grant us the rights and privileges of American citizens, and allow us entry back into our nation. That's what faith does. It entitles us to things we cannot see—things that are a long way off, yet we know deep down are ours. Faith bestows assurance that what we yet hope for will come to fruition.

> Faith is the assurance (the confirmation, the title deed) of the things [we] hope for, being the proof of things [we] do not see and the conviction of their reality [faith perceiving as real fact what is not revealed to the senses] (Hebrews 11:1 AMPC).

A title deed of the things we hope for! Essentially, that means our faith is the official, embossed certificate upon which we stake our claim. The thing we hope for doesn't occur so that we will believe. We believe and *then* it transpires! As Jesus pointed out, our faith actually makes things happen. Two blind men followed Jesus right into the home where He was staying. I can see their canes tapping on the ground as they struggled to keep up with Him. When the Lord asked if they believed He could make them see, they both responded, "Yes, Lord" (Matthew 9:28). And then Scripture records that "he touched their eyes and said, 'Because of your faith, it will happen'" (Matthew 9:29).

Because of their faith, two blind men suddenly were able to see. First we believe, then we will see God do the impossible.

This does not imply that our holy God is a mere genie—that we simply think something will occur, and so it does. It means to believe when we are compelled by His Spirit to stand against the very circumstances tugging our hearts down to the dirt. It means our faith is supernaturally stirred (and oh, thank God for His stirring up and strengthening our faith), which reminds us that when we are in agreement with Him, it will be done for us. It means we can dare to stand against unbelief itself. We don't have to struggle, wondering if what we're longing for is even possible. Jesus assures us, it is!

A Pivotal Choice

When God asks us to do something that feels impossible, or when our road abruptly changes, and a massive chasm appears that stretches between what we long for and what we have, between who we yearn to be and who we are, between what we sense God requiring of us and our stark inability, between the truth of God's promises and the barren reality we face, we have a choice. God graciously bestows an invitation, and it is my fervent prayer that we will not only hear the Lord's stunning invitation, but that we will lay aside all else and accept it with joy.

God is whispering to us, *Will you follow Me if I lead you the hard way? Will you trust Me even when I take you the way you don't want to go? Will you allow My strength to work in your weakness?*

And the kicker: *Will you worship Me in the midst of your suffering?*

Worship shifts our focus onto the One who is able to carry out His purpose, in spite of the chasm, in spite of our inability, in spite of our doubts and fears, and in spite of our pain. He is able to do far above all we can dare to ask or think.

> Now to Him Who, by (in consequence of) the [action of His] power that is at work within us, is able to [carry out His purpose and] do superabundantly, far over and above all that we [dare] ask or think [infinitely beyond our highest prayers, desires, thoughts, hopes, or dreams] (Ephesians 3:20 AMPC).

Infinitely beyond! When our hearts are riveted onto Him, the Lord goes infinitely beyond our highest prayers and thoughts and desires. I've prayed some pretty radical prayers, so the thought of God going beyond even those daring petitions captivates me. It makes me giddy. It makes me realize how much He loves me and how big He is in comparison to all else.

Worship brings us into His comforting, peaceful presence while we face the chasm. It keeps us close to Him so that we never have to be afraid. As Psalm 23:4 reminds us, "Even when I walk through the darkest valley, I will not be afraid, for you are close beside me." How can we possibly entertain fear when He is right next to us?

Worshipping brings His presence into our midst, into the middle of all we are facing. Worship changes our hearts because it invites God in, and where the Spirit of the Lord is, freedom hangs in the very air. "For the Lord is the Spirit, and wherever the Spirit of the Lord is, there is freedom" (2 Corinthians 3:17).

We can embrace freedom from the doubt that we cannot possibly do what He's asking. Freedom from the discouragement that bangs hard against our hearts when it appears nothing is changing. Freedom from every lie that hisses into our brains.

Worship invites God's holy, awesome, mighty presence in. And hills of opposition and doubt and discouragement melt away in His presence. "The mountains melt like wax before the Lord, before the Lord of all the earth" (Psalm 97:5). All our doubts, our fears, our inadequacies evaporate like water on a hot Arizona road.

Worship keeps our focus off of the chasm and on Jesus, Who *is* the chasm-closer. He is the bridge. The door. The way. He makes a way through the crazy. He told us that Himself through the prophet Isaiah:

> I am the Lord, who opened a way through the waters, making a dry path through the sea. I called forth the mighty army of Egypt with all its chariots and horses. I drew them beneath the waves, and they drowned, their lives snuffed out like a smoldering candlewick. But forget all that—it is nothing compared to what I am going to do. For I am about to do something new. See, I have already begun! Do you not see it? *I will* make a pathway through the wilderness. *I will* create rivers in the dry wasteland (Isaiah 43:16-19, italics mine).

I will.

When we cannot, He will. He will make a way where there is no way. He will enable us. He will stand with us and strengthen us. He will fight for us.

Worship declares that we trust God, even as we stare across the chasm of our disappointment, our inability, our grief. Worship shouts that He is worthy of our praise even when we don't know how things are going to work out. I think that when we choose to worship God in the middle of our hard road, it's as close to worshipping Him in Spirit and in truth as we can get.

When Jesus said, "It is finished," He had accomplished through the cross everything that everyone in all of time would ever need. He closed the gaps in our abilities, He supernaturally equipped us. He secured our way to the other side—to eternity—for all eternity.

Regardless of what is before us, whatever God is leading us toward, it is possible because either He will supernaturally enable us, or He will move on our behalf. Whether He is asking us to stay or go, step out or step back, move forward or step aside, speak out or remain silent, we can do it or trust Him to do what we cannot. Because He is the chasm-closer.

Your Personal Proclamation:
SAY IT. KNOW IT. BELIEVE IT.

I walk by faith, not by sight. I know and listen to my Savior's voice and will not listen to the voice of the enemy. I will disregard what I see with my eyes so that I can instead embrace what I am sensing with my heart: God's promise for me in my every situation. I believe God enables me, equips me, and fights for me.

I will allow every obstacle, every chasm I face, to teach and prepare and strengthen and direct my heart. I trust that God is at work on my behalf, and that He will either supernaturally equip me, or He will do the thing I cannot. I will not entertain the enemy's taunts but will yield to the Holy Spirit and engage with my God. I will not allow myself to be disturbed. I will not be faithless any longer. I will believe.

5

For Our Every Meltdown, Freak-Out, and Gut-Wrenching Hurt

I AM YOUR STABILITY

❧

Look! I am placing a foundation stone in Jerusalem, a firm
and tested stone. It is a precious cornerstone that is safe
to build on. Whoever believes need never be shaken.

ISAIAH 28:16

It arrived in the form of a heart-rattling text. Simple, straightforward, and unexpected, it read, "I've got something to tell you." Instinctively, my stomach contracted, and in an instant I knew—I just knew—it wouldn't be good news. That day, through that odd, instant intuition, the Holy Spirit was disclosing to me that something unpleasant would soon unfold.

The Holy Spirit does that for us—discloses to us what is to come. I'm deeply awed and grateful when He guides us, speaks to us, and, in a beautifully protective way, often chooses to reveal what's on the horizon. I believe that in His vast loving-kindness, He does this to prepare us. It's sort of like God enabling us to supernaturally brace ourselves so we don't get sucker-punched.

Sometimes this holy knowing, as I call it, advises us of upcoming change. For me, this has occurred prior to a major geographic relocation, before conceiving our third child, and before I stepped out to begin writing.

Sometimes holy knowing takes the shape of a word of encouragement or confirmation from a friend. I can't tell you how grateful I am for Spirit-led friends who accurately hear what the Holy Spirit is disclosing and speak life to me when I'm in decision-making mode, or even when I simply need encouragement and reassurance. And I rejoice when the Lord reveals something to me that turns out to be a word in due season that I can share with a loved one.

On the particular day of the unexpected text, I had to wait hours and hours before the dreaded conversation took place. Though I sensed something serious was about to hit me, I had no idea what it could be. Still, I tried not to anticipate the worst. Yet a battle ensued in my mind and heart. All of which means I had hours and hours to wonder, fret, and stew.

Determined to at least *attempt* to keep calm, I remained in a state of prayer throughout the day, though I confess it was not calm, sweet, fearless prayer. More like desperate, panicky prayer. The kind that automatically bubbles up even while you're folding the laundry because of the potential crisis you sense looming on the horizon. The kind you pray when you're praying blind. The kind that means business. It was a *Lord help me, prepare me, intervene in whatever this is, establish Your will, and oh God, I need You to be in this* prayer.

As I continued praying, the Holy Spirit brought a verse to my mind. I rushed straight to my Bible, and what I read brought me to tears. It was precisely what I needed to hear.

> You will guard him and keep him in perfect and constant peace whose mind [both its inclination and its character] is stayed on You, because he commits himself to You, leans on You, and hopes confidently in You (Isaiah 26:3 AMPC).

Perfect and constant peace. Isn't that precisely what our very souls long for when we're hit with the unexpected, with the devastating? When everything in us wants to run straight into our bedroom, dive onto our bed, and hide under the covers for the next three weeks, is it actually possible to experience supernatural, authentic, ongoing peace instead? This situation-defying promise radiated right out of my Bible and lodged directly into my heart. It was exactly what I needed, right when I needed it.

Laser-Like Focus

So how exactly do we experience God's perfect and constant peace in the middle of the unknown...whether it's when the storm winds are just beginning to blow and we sense the worst is yet to come, when we've received awful news, or when a worst-case scenario has just emergency-landed right in our living room?

Simply stated, Isaiah 26:3 is a two-part conditional promise, and a portion of the condition rests squarely on us. Our part is simple, though not easy: to keep our minds focused steadfastly on the Lord... even when life goes crazy. Especially when life goes crazy. Not in a *loco* denial-of-facts way, but in an *I trust You, God, and confidently expect You to work as only You can* way.

I never thought I'd quote a martial arts superstar, but this really resonates a powerful truth with me, so here goes: As Bruce Lee puts it, "The successful warrior is the average man, with laser-like focus."

As I grow older, remaining focused on a single task (or a single thought!) has become a bit more challenging. I really have to make a concerted effort not to flit from one thought, idea, or task to another, because mentally the capacity to refocus again after being distracted isn't as easy as when I was in my twenties.

But it's not just the normal aging process that inhibits our focusing skills. We laud the latest technology, but it absorbs our ever increasingly distracted attention. We daily juggle a plethora of nonstop information fire-hosing into our faces via around-the-clock news channels, emails, phone calls, and the constant ding-ding-ding of texting. As social media takes more of our time (and brain cells), multitasking has become the hallmark of our culture, and our ability to focus has weakened considerably.

Two things are at play for many of us: First, because we often live distracted lives, when calamity hits we discover that our deep wells of God's wisdom and refreshing peace are more like shallow cisterns. Lack of focus equals a lack of depth, and we cannot draw out what we have not poured in or allowed God to pour in. Our ability and willing-ness to focus—specifically on God's Word and His promises—directly affects our faith and thus our responses and even our emotions in times of crisis.

Second is the reality of our current troubling circumstance, which of course grabs our attention and refuses to let go. Looking away is a gargantuan task, let alone refocusing on the Lord and His Word, His promises, and His truth.

But if we are to be successful warriors—and you'd better believe our lives absolutely require us to live as warriors—then laser-like focus is mandatory. We can cultivate and practice laser-like focus, but not just focus for focus's sake. We are focusing on the Lord and His truth for the sake of our spiritual growth and maturity, for our ability to stand firm when all hell breaks loose against us, and even for the sake of our sanity!

If we become what we behold, and we constantly stare at the mess before us, heaven help us. But if, by God's grace and holy determina-tion we commit to keeping our focus on Jesus, then we will reap the supernatural benefits of perfect and constant peace...regardless of our mess.

Part two of the condition of Isaiah 26:3 is completely the Lord's responsibility. His part is to usher us into and keep us within His super-natural peace—as we trust in Him and choose to take refuge in Him. He promises to do just that, provided that we do our part by taking refuge in and trusting Jesus and remaining focused on Him instead of whatever awful situation is holding our attention hostage. And He is faithful and utterly trustworthy, and He will do exactly what He has promised (1 Thessalonians 5:24).

But sometimes even when we do our best to remain focused on the Lord, a sudden calamity can appear to be the perfect time to freak out.

To Panic or Not to Panic: That Is the Question

It was a worst-case scenario. Esther, the queen of the Persian Empire, received disturbing news that her cousin Mordecai stood before the king's gate in sackcloth and ashes—grieving attire—crying with a loud and bitter cry (Esther 4:1). It wasn't an unexpected text, but it was a heart-rattling situation. Scripture tells us, "When Esther's maids and her attendants came and told it to her, the queen was exceedingly grieved and distressed" (Esther 4:4 AMPC).

Isn't this exactly what happens to us? When we discover heartrending information, our hearts knot up, and we are exceedingly grieved and distressed. But Esther's ultimate response was one of calm wisdom. Oh, that the Lord would help us to respond in kind!

Esther realized a serious situation was underway but had no idea what it could be. She loved Mordecai, who had taken her in and raised her as his own after her parents died. Years later, when King Ahasuerus divorced the disobedient Queen Vashti, he sought a new wife to replace her, and Esther was one of many beautiful, young virgins brought into the royal harem. Neither Mordecai nor Esther knew she would eventually become the king's chosen new queen, but for now here she was, and there Mordecai stood.

Esther needed to find out what was going on, fast. She sent for one of the king's attendants and ordered him to speak with Mordecai, who brought her what turned out to be deeply troubling news. The entire Jewish population was scheduled to be legally destroyed on a specific date in the not-too-distant future, with the king's blessing, thanks to the evil plan of Haman, the Jew's enemy.

There was just one problem: The king had no idea that his own wife, Esther, was Jewish.

If ever there was a perfect time to panic, this was it.

I've been the recipient of numerous absolutely perfect opportunities to panic, and I've had so many meltdowns I probably deserve some sort of an award. (You might be in the running too.) I've wailed, worried, sweated, dealt with stomachaches, headaches, grouchiness, and the utter inability to sleep. All because panic seemed like a perfectly reasonable option. All because instead of daring to believe God's promises and His never-changing, utterly stabilizing truth, I allowed the circumstances to overwhelm me.

When Panic Seems Logical and Necessary

The day of my heart-rattling text ended with some difficult, weighty conversations concerning a previously unsuspected and quite serious family matter. I hated that the whole scenario was happening late at night (which for me means anything past 9 p.m.). My brain struggled to process everything. The storm of information being disclosed and the hidden facts being brought to light felt overwhelming, and nothing I or anyone else did could alter the truth of these awful new realities.

As the messy truth of my situation unfolded that evening, I could feel myself trembling on the inside. My heart raced. My shoulders rose up to ear level. I struggled to slow my breath, not wanting to hyperventilate in the middle of a family crisis and add a head injury to our troubles. Everything in me wanted to scream, run around in circles, and panic!

That's when Jesus nudged me with a question. Is it just me, or does it seem like Jesus's questions often come at the strangest moments? There I was, on the brink of hyperventilating, brokenhearted, and trying hard not to throw something, when I heard His question loud and clear. He asks this same question of us all in our hardest scenarios—during the hard-to-believe situations that make our insides quiver and our knees tremble: "Why are you afraid? Do you still have no faith?" (Mark 4:40).

Why, indeed. When would I truly understand that my peace and inner stability cannot and must not depend upon my circumstances?

Why do the fierce waves appear to loom larger than our Lord? Yes, the waves are sometimes massive. Yes, our little bitty boats of faith get battered, and sometimes when it's really bad, it looks like we just might sink.

But if Jesus is with us, if He is truly Immanuel, *God with us*, why *are* we afraid? And where, exactly, is our faith when we truly need it?

Jesus is always right there with us. He sees what's going on. He is *never* oblivious to what we're going through. And He is able and willing to either calm the storm or calm our hearts in the midst of the storm. He eventually does one or the other, though sometimes not as immediately as we might prefer. Nor are most of us eager to embrace such rough seasons.

Holy Training Ground

God allows storms and trials and disappointments for many reasons, but the most obvious is this: He is training us. It's sort of like a training journey that we never finish because, girl, I don't know about you, but I am still a hot mess. We all are. We will never be perfect this side of heaven, and yet I still long to live in a way that always honors and pleases the Lord. And so the apostle Paul's prayer must become ours, as well:

> We ask God to give you complete knowledge of his will and to give you spiritual wisdom and understanding. Then the way you live will always honor and please the Lord, and your lives will produce every kind of good fruit. All the while, you will grow as you learn to know God better and better (Colossians 1:9-10).

As much as I wish I learned best while lounging in my fluffy bathrobe, sipping something sweet and delicious, and watching a sappy Hallmark movie, it doesn't work that way (not that God can't speak through a Hallmark movie—or any movie—or while we're wearing our bathrobes). Through the spiritual wisdom and understanding God offers, we can understand that we learn obedience through the hard stuff, the awful stuff, and the flat gut-wrenching things we endure.

Not even Jesus was excluded from this holy training; He learned obedience through the hard things He endured (Hebrews 5:8). If the Savior of the world had to learn obedience (and my guess is, many other things, such as tenacity, dying to Himself, loving the unlovely, and more than we'll probably ever know) through the hard things, won't we, as well?

And because Jesus clearly, willingly submitted to God's holy training, shouldn't we? Do we value having a willing, obedient heart more than our own comfort and ease?

The apostle Paul tells us, "Physical training is good, but training for godliness is much better, promising benefits in this life and in the life to come" (1 Timothy 4:8). And how can we train if we never endure the unexpected, the unbelievable, the unthinkable, the unwanted? One of the many things He is teaching us is to allow Him to help us remain calm in the face of considerable adversity. But it's not something we decide on and then *poof!* we're automatically calm-bots. For some of us, freak-outs will always be that glittery option dangling on the periphery that we must choose to resist.

And of course there are the what-ifs.

Battling the What-Ifs

Esther's cousin Mordecai then asked her the unthinkable: He charged her to go before the king and plead with him for the lives of her people. However, that was no simple task. Esther couldn't just waltz into the throne room. National law stated that *any* person who appeared before the king without an official summons faced the penalty of death (including wives!).

Esther had not been called to the king for thirty days, yet this unthinkable crisis demanded an immediate response. There existed, however, a loophole in the law. If, by the king's mercy, his golden scepter was extended toward the one appearing before the king without an official summons, that person's life would be spared.

But what if that didn't happen? Would the king sentence Esther to death? And what if Haman's devastating plan wasn't stopped?

Why do we allow the what-ifs to torture us? What if instead of entertaining what-ifs, we declared to ourselves who God is (sovereign, majestic, fully able, omnipotent, greater than anything) and what He is capable of (*all* things)? What if we declared (out loud!) that we will no longer allow the what-ifs to freak us out; that we will longer listen to the lies of the enemy, because we hear the voice of the Good Shepherd and follow only Him?

I think that's what Esther did. She refused to entertain the what-ifs, and she immediately took action, deciding two things. She would risk her life and appear unsummoned before the king, consequences faced with head raised. But first, she requested that Mordecai and all the Jews in the city fast for three days, and she and her maids also fasted.

These two decisions reveal a beautiful, noble depth of character.

Mustering her courage, Esther realized she must do the unthinkable. And in order to do that, she knew she must cry out to the Lord for His intervention and favor, without which she would surely die. She risked her very life, but not before putting her life in the hands of the One who reigned sovereign over it all.

When unthinkable situations threaten to rip our hearts right out of us, we would be wise to take Esther's divine strategy to heart and declare a fast. Fasting is the spiritual declaration and recognition of our utter need and dependence upon the Lord. Fasting relinquishes our natural, normal human need for sustenance, and invites Jesus into our situations; it invites Him to become our primary, vital source of strength and stability. And fasting enlarges our foundation. It's the equivalent of stepping off of a rickety, worn-out old porch with missing planks and stepping onto a massive granite boulder—a Solid Rock. The sovereign Lord Almighty is *the* stabilizing force in our lives.

One evening as a fierce thunderstorm rolled in, I snapped a spectacular picture from my driveway. A laser-like ray of sunlight pierced through deep-gray clouds directly over my roof, its beam pointing straight down toward the very center of our home.

God has used this picture to remind me that He is always at work when things look dark. A vital component of our stability in life's shakiest moments rests in knowing this simple truth: God is always at work. Sometimes situations blow in and out of our lives like an intense summer thunderstorm; the winds pick up, lightning flashes, and before we know it we're caught in the deluge. But sometimes storms last a long time, testing our faith and making our hope waver. When it feels like our stormy circumstance won't end, and the winds of pain will never die down, we need to remember God is at work even when things look dark.

In spite of how things appear, when we pray and invite Him into the situation, His magnificent light pierces through the clouds of our circumstances—and that is incredibly comforting to me.

God is inviting us to a whole new level of trust—to believe that He is capable of piercing through our situations. This is the hope we have— that the light and truth and power of God Almighty can penetrate our bleakest circumstance to bring His radiant presence, His hope, and transformation. That no matter how dark things get, His light makes all the difference, and it will shine all the brighter because of the darkness.

No matter how bad the storm becomes, when we pray, we can know—really know—that God is at work in our lives. He grants us stability. The book of Esther clearly reveals God working behind the scenes. How reassuring and comforting! What a breathtaking relief! For a season it appeared evil would prevail, yet the exact opposite happened. The wicked Haman, hater of the Jews, had his evil plans, but God had *His*. And God's plans prevailed.

> The LORD of Heaven's Armies has sworn this oath: "It will all happen as I have planned. It will be as I have decided" (Isaiah 14:24).

Like Esther, we have a choice. We can buckle under the what-ifs, or we can trust that God is at work behind the scenes.

We just need to know how to walk that out.

Shifting the Atmosphere of Our Hearts

If there's one thing I want to know, it's why I often drop my peace like a hot potato when some knee-wobbling occurrence or other happens. I never intend for that to happen, and it usually doesn't take long for me to realize my peace is gone. I'm not sure why it's sometimes so easy to relinquish our peace, but as I thought about all that had happened with the unexpected text scenario, God showed me something.

I understood that the moment I read that text, I made a choice. I had surrendered my peace. I might as well have been facing a holdup with a gun-toting, masked thug, because that's how fast I gave it up. Then God spoke.

Don't ever go where the enemy is trying to drag you. Guard your heart and hold on to your peace.

Now we know the enemy is a thief, and sometimes God allows him to do awful things (just read the book of Job or the current headlines). But he can only take our peace when we allow it...when we willingly surrender it. If we want peace in the middle of our crazy times, we need to hold tight to it for all we're worth. We need to hold tight to our Prince of Peace.

The enemy knows how to rattle us. He knows our weak spots. He knows how we've always reacted in the past. But our response to any of the stuff he's doing or attempting to do in our lives is always, always our choice.

We must refuse—absolutely refuse—to yield our peace. Esther refused to yield her peace. We must stop allowing ourselves to be agitated and disturbed and unsettled (Jesus's own words!).

This means panic is optional. We can choose *not* to panic. We can't always control what life throws our way. But holding on to peace is always a choice.

God literally helps us to remain calm when we face days of adversity:

> Blessed (happy, fortunate, to be envied) is the man whom You discipline and instruct, O Lord, and teach out of Your law, *that You may give him power to keep himself calm in the days of adversity,* until the [inevitable] pit of corruption is dug for the wicked (Psalm 94:12-13 AMPC, italics mine).

We can pray and ask the Lord to help us shift the atmosphere of our hearts by shifting our focus onto Jesus, the Prince of Peace.

Distracted by the Enemy

One of the enemy's primary tactics in our day-to-day lives is distraction, and he does this in some specific ways: through our minds, and through either crisis circumstances or I've-got-to-get-busy circumstances.

If the devil can keep our minds distracted, he can keep our minds off of the truth, off of God's goodness, and out of alignment with God's Word. Then that ungodly focus takes us by the hand and leads us straight to the brink of a meltdown. This happens when we allow our minds to run away with worst-case scenarios or when we allow our to-do lists to boss us around.

That's why God's Word encourages us to think about specific things:

"And now, dear brothers and sisters, one final thing. Fix your thoughts on what is true, and honorable, and right, and pure, and lovely, and admirable. Think about things that are excellent and worthy of praise" (Philippians 4:8).

This doesn't mean we completely ignore and daydream away serious issues that require our attention and prayer. It doesn't mean we avoid our responsibilities. It's a holy reminder not to allow ourselves to dwell in negativity and assume the worst. It's a wise admonition from the Lord to keep our minds focused on Him, even when our to-do list is as long as our arm.

If the enemy can distract us through circumstances, we can feel far too overloaded, overwhelmed, and overcome to focus. It's a distraction ploy that often occurs when an unexpected crisis hits, or even when all the busyness of life continually fire-hoses into our faces.

Recently, I realized what a fight and a struggle it is each morning to just stop and sit before the Lord. Minute after minute my brain tells me all the things I need to do. Distractions holler. And yet as I discipline myself, as I shush every wayward thought and refuse to give in to the busyness of my mind, I am rewarded. His beautiful, faithful presence greets me. As I spend time that I'm tempted to believe I don't have, He revives me. He strengthens me. He stabilizes me. And every single morning that I choose to meet with Jesus, my jangled heart is recalibrated and settled and softly prepared for the day ahead of me.

We are not women given to distraction, but women who dare to believe God. We believe He is greater, He is able, and He will stabilize us. The very moment we recognize the enemy is at work to distract us through attacking our minds or through circumstances, we must run to the Lord, and we must pray. Over and over. Morning, noon, and night.

He promises to hear us. If there's anything that irks me, it's when I pour out my heart to someone who doesn't seem to hear. It's like they're listening but not really. God never does that. Never. He doesn't have something more important to rush off to. He doesn't need a break from us. He's there, arms open, eager to embrace us and listen to every word.

It's okay to vent and complain to the Lord. I think sometimes we feel we have to maintain a measure of propriety with the Lord, but just look at how David processed his emotions through the Lord in the Psalms!

We're emotional. We can groan and sigh and moan with the best of them. And that's okay. We're human. God gave us emotions, and while we shouldn't allow them to run our entire lives, it's good and healthy and wise for us to submit every one of them to the Lord and ask Him to settle and stabilize our hearts and emotions. That's what David did. Through the Psalms we are encouraged to run to the Lord and share the deepest needs of our hearts.

> When I choose to meet with Jesus, my jangled heart is recalibrated and settled.

David understood that when we release our emotions and troubling circumstances to the Lord, He sustains us and stabilizes us.

> Cast your burden on the Lord [releasing the weight of it] and He will sustain you; He will never allow the [consistently] righteous to be moved (made to slip, fall, or fail) (Psalm 55:22 AMPC).

God sees what's happening. He hears our prayers. And by the power of His mighty Holy Spirit, He will sustain and stabilize us.

Stop and Then

One of the vital keys to remaining calm when adversity swoops in is to *stop and then.*

We can choose to stop obsessing, stop worrying, stop allowing ourselves to be agitated and disturbed, and stop fixating on the problem, *and then* we can choose to worship the Lord Who is above all things, Who is able to do exceedingly abundantly above all that we ever dared to hope or imagine, Who loves us with an everlasting love, and Who strengthens us with His joy.

It might sound flat crazy, but trust me on this. Worshipping right smack in the middle of the ugly, the crazy, the you-have-got-to-be-kidding, literally shifts the atmosphere of our hearts. And when the winds kick up and the dark clouds roll in, we *need* the atmosphere to shift. We need to see a ray of His holy sunlight piercing into our homes and into our aching hearts.

But what if we don't have a song in us? What if the very spark of worship has been sucked out of us? What then?

We can stop and then dwell on His Word. We can stop and then meditate on God's promises, constantly reminding ourselves of His goodness and that He is at work behind the scenes. We stop and then open our hearts to the Lord, reaching out to Him, processing our pain through Him, just like David did (read the book of Psalms if you need inspiration!). And then? We can stop and ask the Lord to put a song in our hearts.

He will.

Can't Touch This

One of the best things God ever said to me was at one of my absolute worst moments. Life as I knew it was collapsing around me, and my stunned heart struggled to understand. Even breathing seemed a monumental accomplishment. Then the Lord spoke.

I have deprived it of power to harm you.

Those nine words poured a stunning, holy truth into my desperate heart. They are the words of Christ as recorded in John 16:33:

> I have told you these things, so that in Me you may have [perfect] peace and confidence. In the world you have tribulation and trials and distress and frustration; but be of good cheer [take courage; be confident, certain, undaunted]! For I have overcome the world. [*I have deprived it of power to harm you* and have conquered it for you] (AMPC, italics mine).

What that meant to me was that even though my gargantuan circumstances felt undefeatable, even though I hated every step of what I was walking through, even though it was excruciating and I loathed every moment, ultimately, it could not permanently harm me.

Jesus would not allow it.

That doesn't mean we won't endure hurts and won't have scars. It means the very thing that Satan intended to inflict permanent harm on our souls has been deprived of its power. Yes, we face frustration and distress and trials—colossal trials—but we can dare to be of good cheer anyway, knowing that Jesus has secured our victory, if not in the immediate here and now (and let's face it, life can be so hard, and we endure much heartache) then in eternity. Because He has overcome, we can overcome.

When unexpected, excruciating events hit hard, our first response should be to run to the Lord. He will always do two things: He will speak peace to our hearts, and He will give us divine strategy. The Lord is gracious and compassionate. He is slow to anger and abounding in loving-kindness (Psalm 145:8). He desires to speak to our hearts, to reassure us, and to give us wisdom and insight.

As we train our hearts to hear His voice by running to Him every single time we are in need—when we need discernment, when we're puzzled, when we need wisdom, when calamity hits—He will bring exactly what we need. He will soothe us with His presence. Every answer comes from Him. And He always provides.

I am not advocating running to the Lord only when a crisis hits, but training ourselves to always go to Him with every concern or need. This is how God becomes our stability. This is how we remain calm in the midst of adversity. This is how, when everything around us is violently shaken, we are not. We are supernaturally steadied. Because He is with us, we are not shaken.

Your Personal Proclamation:
SAY IT. KNOW IT. BELIEVE IT.

The Lord is my stability. I will not allow myself to be agitated and disturbed. I will not relinquish my peace, but I will anchor myself to Jesus, my Prince of Peace. I will abide in Him. Though my situation might not change immediately or work out exactly the way I hoped, I dare to believe that God is at work, and that He is faithful and trustworthy.

The waves and the chaos will not overtake me because Jesus is my Rock and stability. He enables me to remain calm in days of adversity. I will not be distracted but will focus on God's promises: His peace is mine, He is my shield, His purposes for me will stand, and He has deprived this world of the power to harm me. He is my stability.

6

Knocking Knees Aside
YOU ARE BRAVE

*I tell you, you can pray for anything, and if you
believe that you've received it, it will be yours.*

MARK 11:24

I shivered. Goosebumps covered my arms and legs, but not from the temperature. I sat stone still, my seven-year-old brain struggling as frightening images flashed across the school movie screen. I watched, breathless, as a strange man in a dark suit lured a pretty little girl, probably my age, toward his car.

I held my breath as the movie played out, horrified that the little girl wearing the cute navy dress was suddenly a bloody, mangled mess. My heart filled with panic. I could feel my pulse hammering. When the film was over, and the lights came back on, I glanced around the school auditorium, suddenly suspicious of any man wearing a suit—of any man at all. Would one of them come after me too? Would I be able to get home from school safely?

All this inner drama stemmed from a so-called safety film my entire school watched. Ostensibly warning the student body of stranger danger way back in 1968, its violent scenes had gone too far—at least for my sensitive heart—and I had felt anything *but* safe for a single second ever since.

That night, the brutal images flashed in my mind. Already emotionally insecure because of the tumultuous atmosphere of our home, that dreadful safety film shook the flimsy foundation of security I knew, leaving an all-too-keen awareness of my own vulnerability. Why, at any moment a stranger might abduct me. Over and over I saw the scenes, the innocent little girl who foolishly took a fatal ride with a stranger; her face a flat, mangled, bloody warning to us all. Fear had planted its devious little seed, and at the time I could hardly begin to understand its ramifications.

I shifted into hypervigilance mode, constantly and carefully screening situations, people, places—all in an effort to protect myself and remain safe, all done out of fear. From that moment on, no matter how hard I tried, I often felt unsafe. Evil was out there, and if I didn't remain vigilant, it might get me.

Since I never spoke to my parents (or anyone) about my fears, I lacked perspective, wisdom, and the balance of truth, and those fears had ample time to take deep root in my heart. This, coupled with my father's erratic rage issues, fostered a need for me to remain almost permanently on guard. Unnatural alertness took the place of the calm normal in which we're supposed to live. It was like sharing a house with an occasionally nice thug who walked around with a club behind his back.

From a young girl's irrational fears of abduction to more complex adult ones, like the fear of my most basic needs not being met (check), fears no one would love me (check), fears I wasn't like or nearly as good as everyone else (check check), I lived and breathed fear on countless levels.

But after becoming a believer, and as I matured in Christ, I began to gain a holy understanding of how fear works.

Fear's Modus Operandi

If you've ever experienced a bully's torment or remember watching a kid lose his lunch money to a bully back when you were in grade school, then believe it or not, you're already familiar with one of fear's tactics.

That's right. Fear is a bully.

And just like a tough, mean kid staring you down in the school hallway, fear wants to intimidate you and prevent you from moving forward. But that's not all.

Those thoughts you occasionally have? They're not always you. Sometimes the enemy screams his bully taunts to intimidate us: *You'll never be able to do that. You're pathetic. You are not qualified, so you might as well stop right now.*

Unfortunately, sometimes what fear screams is completely true. We really *did* do that awful thing. We did lose it big-time. We did sin over and over and over. We all miss the mark. As James 3:2 puts it, "We all often stumble and fall and offend in many things" (AMPC).

If the enemy can—through fear—keep our eyes glued to our mistakes, our bad choices, and our past, then he wins. The enemy wants to bully us right into a corner and extract every penny of faith from our pockets.

The devil uses fear to imply that we aren't good enough. Well, we aren't. We can never be good enough. But Jesus Christ *is*. The finished work of the cross is all we need; it is our final and only defense.

When the enemy relentlessly shoves our past and our failures into our faces, we must relentlessly remember that once we have confessed our sins to the Lord, He is faithful to forgive us and cleanse us of all unrighteousness (1 John 1:9). His forgiveness is not temporary, but permanent, and He goes so far as to remove our sins from us once and for all (Psalm 103:12).

Secondly, though our past and current failures may make us wince on the inside, God has beautifully ordained that each one is ultimately part of our triumph. In the way only He can, the Lord uses what the enemy means for our harm and turns it all around for good. For eternity.

The glaring sins that the enemy hurls back into our faces turn into our powerful testimonies that point those around us to Jesus. Our testimonies not only showcase God's love, power, and faithfulness to a lost and dying world, these same testimonies also remind us that we have no need to fear, that our place with Him is secure and eternal.

And yet there is another component at work.

Fear Is a Spirit

Fear, which the Scripture verse below exposes as a spirit, succeeds in working against us in myriad ways—at times more subtle, and at times no holds barred:

> God did not give us a spirit of timidity (of cowardice, of craven and cringing and fawning fear), but [He has given us a spirit] of power and of love and of calm and well-balanced mind and discipline and self-control (2 Timothy 1:7 AMPC).

As we dissect this verse, we can begin to discern many of the ways fear works against us.

Fear yanks our minds out of balance. It magnifies potential worst-case scenarios until we're absolutely convinced of the worst. Suddenly, the issue we're facing looms so large in our minds that we decide we cannot possibly face or defeat it. Our best response is to instead magnify the Lord through worship until He restores divine perspective.

Fear causes us to cringe on the inside, making us feel timid, feeble, weak, and inept. Actually, we often are exactly that. Yet in a holy paradigm shift, God uses our inabilities to showcase His power. Though I cannot claim to understand it completely, I'm grateful that in spite of my inabilities in general and my fears in particular, God works best in my weakness. The apostle Paul wrote, "I am glad to boast about my weaknesses, so that the power of Christ can work through me" (2 Corinthians 12:9).

We don't have to feel strong to be strong because when we dare to believe Him, the Lord works through us in spite of how we feel.

> We can never be good enough. But Jesus Christ is.

Fear also prevents us from walking in discipline and self-control. How? Fear convinces us it's not worth the effort and not worth pressing on, and *poof!* our desire and discipline evaporate because what's the use? Fear wages war with our inner selves, so instead of discerning the truth about what we hear and controlling our responses, we relent and give up.

Fear's primary tactic is to make us shrink back (in fear) by magnifying the circumstance, the issue, or the person we're currently dealing with. Yet, Scripture tells us that when we shrink back, God takes no delight in us:

> But the just shall live by faith [My righteous servant shall live by his conviction respecting man's relationship to God and divine things, and holy fervor born of faith and conjoined with it]; *and if he draws back and shrinks in fear, My soul has no delight or pleasure in him* (Hebrews 10:38 AMPC, italics mine).

Let this serve as a holy warning to us. Because when we allow fear to intimidate us into shrinking back, we're declaring that God is not enough—that He is not big enough, faithful enough, or able.

. God is more than enough. He is more than able. He supplies all of our needs (Philippians 4:19), He is good (Psalm 136:1), nothing is too difficult for Him (Jeremiah 32:27), and His plans and purposes for us will always stand (Isaiah 46:10).

Language Lessons

When I began learning to speak basic Spanish back in high school, it helped that a close friend at the time spoke it fluently. At her house, where I hung out a lot, Spanish TV shows blared, Spanish music cranked out of the radio, and the entire family spoke Spanish all day long.

Immersed in that atmosphere, I caught on quickly, and it wasn't long before I became almost completely fluent.

Unfortunately, I was also familiar with another language—only I didn't realize it.

I find it fascinating that Scripture reveals that when the devil whispers a lie, he is actually speaking in his native language. His language of origin is not Spanish. Not French. Not English.

The devil speaks Lie.

> For you are the children of your father the devil, and you love to do the evil things he does. He was a murderer from the beginning. He has always hated the truth, because there

is no truth in him. When he lies, it is consistent with his character; for he is a liar and the father of lies (John 8:44).

But that's not all.

The enemy wants *us* to become fluent in his native language as well. He desires for us to become familiar enough with his malevolent language that we recognize it, understand it, and even start to speak it.

Things are never going to change.

God is disappointed in me.

There's no point in trying, and there's no hope for the future.

I get this weird feeling I'm on the brink of a cataclysmic event that's going to ruin my life.

Fear merges with lies in an all-out assault to immobilize us. Freak us out. Get our minds entirely off of God.

Now I'm not implying that all fear is a lie. Healthy fears exist, and we should respect them. Not stepping too close to the edge of a steep cliff is wise. Staying out of a pond where alligators lurk is a good choice.

But if we've become entirely too fluent in Lie, what can we do?

The first and most powerful key in combatting Lie is to become fluent in God's Word—absorb it, ponder it, meditate on it, memorize it, and pray it out loud. This is a vital, important component of pursuing Jesus, who *is* the truth; Jesus is the Word made flesh (John 1:14). As we progress in familiarizing ourselves with the authentic, it immunizes our hearts against the counterfeit—Satan's lies.

We must also ask the Holy Spirit to grant us the ability to recognize when we're on the verge of accepting a lie as truth. With His discernment, we will develop a more critical and accurate inner ear to know and recognize truth and to reject the enemy's lies.

Aside from commonsense fear, the only fear that should regularly influence our lives is the fear of God, which is a deep, reverential awe and recognition of His omnipotence. This fear of God displaces all other fears, because perfect love (and God *is* love) casts out fear.

> Such love has no fear, because perfect love expels all fear. If we are afraid, it is for fear of punishment, and this shows

that we have not fully experienced his perfect love (1 John 4:18).

So we see that God's perfect, unfailing love, operating in and through us, prevails over fear. Every time. Fear cannot win when we dare to embrace and walk in the love of God.

A Picture of Courage

The daughters of Zelophehad—Mahlah, Noah, Hoglah, Milcah, and Tirzah—made a daring, unconventional, and bold decision to stand up for what they believed in. These brave sisters flexed their courage and ended up changing the course of history and, ultimately, the law under which the Israelites lived.

At the end of the 40-year wilderness journey (detailed in the book of Numbers), with the Promised Land on the horizon and the process of land division starting among the tribes of Israel, the sisters realized they stood to lose all of their father's potential and rightful inheritance simply because they were women. Because their father had no sons, Mahlah, Noah, Hoglah, Milcah, and Tirzah decided to challenge the status quo rather than lose their inheritance. So these five audacious women created a petition and, in a massive step of heroic courage, presented it to Moses, Eleazar the priest, the tribal leaders, and the entire community.

Scripture does not detail the private conversations that took place among the sisters as they pulled together their case, but I wonder if fear hammered at their hearts. Was one of the sisters chief at the helm, convincing the others this was the right course to take? I wonder if they vacillated and argued as they considered, prayed, then wrote and rewrote their petition. One thing is certain: By the time the petition was complete, they clearly stood in unity, and they were willing to fight for their legal inheritance.

At a time when women did not traditionally inherit their father's wealth, they boldly stood up and pleaded their case anyway, asking for what they considered to be their due portion. These sisters understood their rights and their place as their father's daughters—his only heirs—and they were not about to allow their portions to go unclaimed. Though fear might have made their knees knock, they determined to go before the chieftains and Moses himself with backs straight and heads held high.

The Amplified Bible says it this way: *Then came the daughters of Zelophehad.* The atmosphere shifted when these five stepped forward. And God noticed.

Before the entire assembly, Mahlah, Noah, Hoglah, Milcah, and Tirzah laid out their case:

> "Our father died in the wilderness," they said. "But he was not among Korah's followers, who rebelled against the LORD; he died because of his own sin. But he had no sons. Why should the name of our father disappear from his clan just because he had no sons? Give us property along with the rest of our relatives" (Numbers 27:3-4).

Guess what? God agreed with them!

> The LORD replied to Moses, "The claim of the daughters of Zelophehad is legitimate. You must give them a grant of land along with their father's relatives. Assign them the property that would have been given to their father. And give the following instructions to the people of Israel: If a man dies and has no son, then give his inheritance to his daughters" (Numbers 27:6-8).

God answered their legitimate claim. He does the same for us.

But when was the last time we dared to take such a stand? Have we ever? Have we ever had the guts to believe what God's Word declares and to act upon it with boldness? When was the last time we asked God to strengthen our hearts so we could dare to do what we sense He is calling us to? And when was the last time we dared to stand up to our circumstances, the enemy, or our own doubts and declare our rightful inheritance? Our legitimate claim is our faith—the finished work of the cross and all Christ accomplished for us—and the unique promises God offers every one of us.

Scripture helps shape our requests, giving us both encouragement and parameters when we ask. James 4:2-3 tells us, "You don't have what you want because you don't ask God for it. And even when you ask, you don't get it because your motives are all wrong—you want only what will give you pleasure."

We have not because either 1) we fail to ask, or 2) our reasons are wrong. But we don't have to allow fear to prevent us from asking. In fact, Jesus encouraged us to ask repeatedly. "Keep on asking, and you will receive what you ask for. Keep on seeking, and you will find. Keep on knocking, and the door will be opened to you" (Matthew 7:7).

Do we understand our rights and benefits as daughters of the Most High God? Psalm 103 tells us to *forget not all His benefits.*

What benefits? They are many! This psalm names several:

- He forgives all our sins.
- He heals all our diseases.
- He redeems us from death.
- He crowns us with love and tender mercies.
- He fills our lives with good things.
- He renews our youth (strength).

Our courage grows and even flourishes when we remember all of the stunning benefits God lavishly and graciously provides. When we remember that He is for us, not against us. When we remember that nothing can separate us from His love, that His mercies endure forever, that He is faithful and utterly trustworthy, and that He will never, ever leave us.

His peace—which cannot coexist with fear—is legally and officially ours. Jesus lawfully bequeathed His peace to us. It is ours for the taking. He left it to us just as surely as our grandparents left us the good silver. Peace is our rightful inheritance!

> Peace I leave with you; My [own] peace I now give and bequeath to you. Not as the world gives do I give to you. Do not let your hearts be troubled, neither let them be afraid.

[Stop allowing yourselves to be agitated and disturbed; and
do not permit yourselves to be fearful and intimidated and
cowardly and unsettled.] (John 14:27 AMPC).

But there is a catch. We must choose His peace. Even when it makes
no sense. Smack between *Straight crazy!* and *You've got to be kidding*, we
can breathe in peace and exhale fear. We can stop allowing ourselves
to be fearful. This means that when fear shows up, we don't accommodate it or entertain it. We can turn away from fear and embrace the
Prince of Peace.

Unlike Zelophehad's daughters, we no longer live under Old Testament law but under the finished work of the cross. Our petitions go
straight to God. We simply pray and then dare to believe God's promises, knowing that He loves to provide all that
we need. God rewards our boldness. He agrees
with our legitimate requests and, in fact, has
blessed us with every blessing in the heavenly
realm.

> Have we
> ever had
> the guts to
> believe what
> God's Word
> declares
> and to act
> upon it with
> boldness?

By his divine power, God has given us
everything we need for living a godly life.
We have received all of this by coming to
know him, the one who called us to himself by means of his marvelous glory and
excellence (2 Peter 1:3).

Our Inheritance Will Sometimes Be Challenged

Imagine awakening one ordinary morning, pouring a cup of hot
tea, and preparing some toast with butter and peach jam. Just as you
start to sip and chew, you look out the back window, and something
unusual catches your eye. A strange tent is pitched in the corner of your
backyard. Only you didn't camp out there last night, and neither did
anyone in your entire family. In fact, the tent doesn't look familiar at all.

It does not belong there.

Would you simply continue to sip and chew, or would you call for your husband? Or call 9-1-1? Or march outside to figure out what, exactly, was going on? Of all the options and responses I can think of, the one I would never consider is just to ignore the rogue tent and go on with my day. I would not allow that tent to stay there. In a million years, that would never happen.

But isn't that exactly what happens when we allow the enemy to torment us through his lies and his manipulation concerning our current events, our deepest hopes, and our worst fears? We cower, let things remain, refuse to challenge the lies. We ingest the lies because we don't know better, because we're not fans of conflict, or because we feel weak and inadequate.

We ignore the encroaching tent.

Satan is a rogue tent-pitcher. He's an accuser and a squatter. A trespasser. Yet he can continue to trespass only if we allow it. Unfortunately, I have been guilty of doing just that. Maybe it's because my temperament can sometimes be more passive, or I lean more toward introvert, or maybe it's because I haven't always chosen to be brave. Standing up to the enemy is not my favorite thing.

But standing up to the enemy is a necessary thing. And we do that by living spiritually alert and aware, constantly remembering who we are in Christ, and by knowing our sacred rights as God's beloved, treasured daughters.

We cannot allow our rightful portions to go unclaimed.

God told Moses that the request of the daughters of Zelophehad was just. He sided with Mahlah, Noah, Hoglah, Milcah, and Tirzah, and in so doing, He affirmed their boldness.

Are we as willing to stop the enemy's trespassing and stand up for our rightful inheritance? What are we waiting for?

Choosing Courage

Did you know that, according to Scripture, in the end cowards face the same penalty as unbelievers, murderers, and those who practice witchcraft? It's a surprising, harsh truth. Revelation 21:8 assures us that "their fate is in the fiery lake of burning sulfur. This is the second death."

Why? Why are mere cowards lumped together with (gasp)

murderers? In my mind, murder is far more heinous and serious; the two appear miles apart on the sin continuum. And liars? Liars are plainly several degrees worse than ordinary cowards, right?

Clearly, that's not how God sees it.

Essentially, cowardice and fear are a form of unbelief. It would appear that cowardice and believers are at opposite ends of the faith spectrum. The implication is that believers, by their very nature, believe. They believe God.

But cowards believe fear. They bow down to fear, and fear squelches faith. Fear says, *This is bigger.* Faith says, *God is.* Fear says, *This is impossible.* Faith says, *With God all things are possible.* Fear shouts, *Don't even try.* Faith declares, *I can do all things through Christ.*

Cowards shrink God. Make Him smaller than whatever they're facing. Cowards don't believe. They don't believe God is greater, stronger, or able. Cowards walk in unbelief. Unbelief signifies a serious lack of acquaintance with and trust in Almighty God. And unbelief blocks God's promises. It shuts us out.

> Fear shouts, Don't even try. Faith declares, I can do all things through Christ.

When we choose courage, we choose faith. We choose to believe God, knowing that He sees and rewards our efforts. When we dare to courageously trust the Lord, He rewards our efforts and brings to pass His purposes for us.

The daughters of Zelophehad did not allow themselves to be persuaded against what their hearts told them. But sometimes, unfortunately, we do that very thing.

I Would, But…

How many times have we gladly received a specific promise from God, but then something occurs that, in our eyes, negates or at the very least strongly interferes with that specific promise? We've all dealt with the *buts*—those pesky particulars that interfere by stepping between what *could* happen except for (fill in the blank). The *buts* like to make an intimidating appearance, virtually demanding we relinquish the very thing we so desire.

I wanted to go where I thought God was leading me, but I lost my nerve.

I had hoped that particular relationship would improve, but I realized some people never change.

I wanted to learn to hear God's voice, but I got scared of what He might say.

I desired to trust that God would heal my marriage, but it was just too hard.

Buts are the direct result of magnifying a circumstance and shrinking God. They frustrate God's plans by implying He couldn't possibly provide or move or change the situation. *Buts* are insulting excuses and a slap in the face of the Mighty God for whom nothing is impossible.

I Am Well Able

Caleb, a warrior of great faith, faced down the *buts* and won. An Israeli contingent scouted the Promised Land to provide a report for the eagerly awaiting people (see Numbers 13). Unfortunately, though it was indeed a land of milk and honey, ten of the twelve scouts feared what they saw and crumbled. Convinced they were no match for the giants living in the land, they announced their lopsided, fearful statement, provoking fear among the people.

But Caleb knew otherwise. Well-acquainted with the Lord's ability and willing to believe Him in spite of what he saw, Caleb possessed something the other ten scouts lacked: divine perspective. He knew that the Promised Land was their rightful inheritance and was not about to let the *buts* interfere. So he went before Moses and said, "Let's go at once to take the land…We can certainly conquer it!" (Numbers 13:30).

The enemy will attempt to talk us out of our rightful inheritance. There the Israelites stood on the brink of all God had promised them, yet fear persuaded them that God was no match for what they faced.

Divine perspective stops the *buts*. It changes everything. Divine perspective creates a holy perspective shift that enables us to see from a higher vantage point than humanly possible. It enabled Caleb to see that the towering giants in the land were no match for the Lord. And it allows us to see our situations through the eyes of faith too. We begin to understand that with God, we can do anything. As the psalm proclaims, "In your strength I can crush an army; with my God I can scale any wall" (Psalm 18:29).

What if this became our mantra? Our life motto? Our constant prayer? The thing we repeat to ourselves over and over, instead of kowtowing to the *buts?*

In Your strength, I can.

In Your strength, I can keep going.

In Your strength, I can not only face this situation but soar in the midst of it.

In Your strength, I can stand against fear, hold my head high, and persevere.

Divine perspective enables us to see outside of our limited, feeble scope. It puts doubt and discouragement and fear in its proper place. Through it we can dare to say—aloud—*I am well able!*

Embrace Brave

Bravery has ripple effects. We rarely consider this (at least I don't) because we're so caught up in the everyday and the here and now. Life's daily battles are intense, and sometimes it's all we can do to remain focused and keep plowing forward. Yet our courageous choices act as a gleaming machete, slicing a path through the thick jungle of fear that entangles and trips. Choosing brave helps us fully believe and embrace and pursue God's promises while inspiring those around us and making a way for those behind us.

When young David strode past the quaking-in-their-boots Israelite army, daring to cross the vast, open field where the defiant Goliath towered, he not only slew a nine-and-a-half-foot beast, but his courage rippled through the entire Israelite army. David's fearless valor enabled the Israelites to slaughter and defeat the Philistines that day (see 1 Samuel 17).

When Shadrach, Meshach, and Abednego bravely defied the king's command and refused to bow down to Nebuchadnezzar's golden statue (see the book of Daniel, chapter 3), God rewarded them by supernaturally sparing their lives. The courageous young men stood against what was wrong and obeyed God. Like Zelophehad's daughters, they chose brave.

Who says we can't likewise embrace bravery and inspire others and forge a path? Why shouldn't we step out in courage and create a promising ripple?

A key component in learning to embrace bravery is praying brave prayers—prayers that focus less on avoiding fear or keeping fear away from us and more on courage and confidence and holy mettle. Though we might not always feel fearless, by praying for specific qualities from Scripture, we can fear *less*.

- Instead of praying that fear will be far from us, we can pray for strong, bold, and very courageous hearts (see Joshua 1:9) when fear comes near.

- Instead of asking God to remove all the sources of fear in our lives, we can pray for His grace to run toward the big, scary things with great courage (see 1 Samuel 17:48).

- Instead of praying that fear will leave us alone, we can pray that when we *are* afraid, we will have confidence and trust in and put our reliance on God (see Psalm 56:3).

- Instead of asking God for all fear in our lives to vanish, we can pray that His peace that surpasses all understanding will guard our hearts and minds in Christ Jesus—and supersede all fear (see Philippians 4:6-7).

- Instead of feeling alone and fearful, we can pray to consistently remember God is with us, and we don't have to fear. King David declared, "The Lord is for me, so I will have no fear" (see Psalm 118:6).

I think I need to write the above verse on a sticky-note and attach it to my forehead. If I had it my way, I'd never wrestle with fear again. It would be completely and permanently eradicated from my life (Can I get an amen?). But this side of eternity, I don't know how realistic that goal is. I think we will all have times when we must battle fear, but it is always for a purpose.

Facing down fear teaches us how to engage the enemy, to fight, to stand, and to prevail. So be beautifully clothed in His mighty strength and the holy dignity He lavishly provides. Laugh without a care, free from fear's taunts and digs. I see us—hot messes though we may yet be—laughing beautiful, musical laughs, heads tossed back, and hearts lifted toward heaven because we have nothing to fear.

Your Personal Proclamation:
SAY IT. KNOW IT. BELIEVE IT.

I will not fear because God is with me. I will not allow fear to yank my mind out of balance and magnify my difficult circumstances. I will not allow fear to steal my peace or make me cringe on the inside. I will not shrink back in fear but will live by faith. I will live spiritually alert and aware and stand up to the enemy in God's strength.

I will become a picture of courage by daring to believe God's Word and acting upon it with boldness. I will consistently walk in the sacred peace which is legally mine. I will run toward the big, scary things with the courage God provides. In His strength I am well able to fight, to stand, and to persevere. I have a strong, bold, very courageous heart because God is always with me. I will always, always choose to embrace brave.

7

Because Every Iota of You Matters

YOU ARE SIGNIFICANT

[Most] blessed is the man who believes in, trusts in, and relies on the Lord, and whose hope and confidence the Lord is.

JEREMIAH 17:7 AMPC

It started as the teeniest of seeds, planted quietly, as all seeds are. Finding rich, fertile ground, it sprouted in silence, roots thriving and reaching deep, until they grew robust and entwined, becoming one with my psyche. And like an oak tree planted too near the driveway, it grew undetected until one day mighty roots stabbed through. That was the day God revealed that at the very core of my being there existed a subconscious, inaccurate inner default I had accepted as fact:

I was completely insignificant.

My experiences had taught me that my thoughts and opinions did not matter. It's inherently unfair that lies frequently begin in childhood when we're defenseless, unaware, and unable to discern truth or stand against them. But that's often when the enemy starts what turns out to be a calculated attack on our lives.

If you don't think the enemy plans attacks against us, consider the following Scripture verses:

- When we're advised to remain aware and vigilant, there's a good reason. "Stay alert! Watch out for your great enemy, the devil. He prowls around like a roaring lion, looking for someone to devour" (1 Peter 5:8).

- Remember after Jesus's birth, when Herod Antipas ordered the death of every infant boy, age two and under? That was definitely the enemy working through Herod, seeking to stop God's plan. "Herod was furious when he realized that the wise men had outwitted him. He sent soldiers to kill all the boys in and around Bethlehem who were two years old and under, based on the wise men's report of the star's first appearance" (Matthew 2:16).

- And in the first chapter of Job, we see Satan, the accuser, intently looking throughout the earth, searching for an opportunity to do evil. "Satan answered the LORD, 'I have been patrolling the earth, watching everything that's going on'" (Job 1:7).

- Finally, Jesus outright reveals to Peter that Satan has major plans against him. "Simon, Simon, Satan has asked to sift each of you like wheat" (Luke 22:31).

Clearly none of us is immune from the enemy's systematically planned attacks. He schemes against us, intending to stop God's plans in, for, and through us. A primary scheme he uses is to convince us that we are utterly insignificant. Here are two strategies he employs.

The *When I Do *This* I'm Important* Lie

My gram knelt on the blue shag carpeting in her living room, carefully cutting a light blue polyester fabric upon which she had pinned a McCall's pattern. I sat cross-legged on the gold and white floral sofa across from her, watching.

That day her best friend, Pat, who lived directly across the street, was flying home after being out of town. Gram was driving to the airport to pick her up, and as she expertly snipped the fabric, we talked about airports and flying in general. I had flown down to live with relatives in Arkansas the year prior, and Gram and Boopa had taken a flight to Acapulco for a rare vacation. A photo of them looking giddy, Gram wearing an oversized sombrero, rested on a side table. As we reminisced, my gram sighed.

"I love traveling," Gram said, leaning back onto her heels to look at me, her blue eyes shining. "I always feel so important when I fly."

Even at 14, I thought it a remarkable statement. Of course, back then flying wasn't nearly as common as it is now, and folks actually dressed up when they traveled, so on that level I understood. But still I considered it an odd remark, because my gram was the heart of her home, and in my eyes, an accomplished woman.

A master seamstress, she sewed for herself, her family, and anyone else who asked. She cooked delightful homemade meals, baked a spectacular assortment of Christmas cookies each year, and the entire family spent every holiday in her home. She also put up the world's best strawberry freezer jam and hosted pinochle games on many a Friday night.

But apparently she never felt as truly important as when she was decked out and sitting on an airplane. After all, important people took airplanes to important places. Our brief conversation offered a rare glimpse inside my gram's heart. She felt significant when she was doing something she considered important.

I think many of us feel the same way.

It's tempting to rate our tasks and gauge our inner worth from them. But we must not fall into the snare of believing that we are more or less valuable depending on what we currently find ourselves doing. If our task is in obedience to the Lord, then no undertaking is unimportant, nor are we less so, even while we perform the most menial task.

Do we rank our sense of self on our tasks or events? If we base our sense of significance upon what we're currently doing, then we tread on flimsy ground. It's not about how our responsibilities or activities rate; it's about understanding and truly embracing our intrinsic God-given value.

The *If I'm Busy Then I Matter* Lie

Achieving multiple things on any given day makes me feel

productive, accomplished, useful, and—there's no denying it—significant. And that's not necessarily bad. I like completing the work God assigns to me, and I enjoy the satisfying joy of a job well done. However, when mere *nonstop* becomes our benchmark for significance, we've fallen into the never-ending black hole of busyness as a measure of our worth.

Our culture practically worships busyness, and it seems that busyness has become an acceptable form of assessing our personal importance. We subconsciously think, *If I'm busy, I'm necessary, and therefore I matter.*

When our sense of self-worth depends on our accomplishments, then we rely on a never-ending, ever-expanding task list to prove ourselves. And that does two things: It reduces our value to our abilities and productivity (which, on a side note, also leads to exhaustion), and it diminishes us to mere human doings instead of human beings.

That has never been God's plan. We are significant not because of all we do but because we are His. He knows us and cares about what concerns us, and He loves us with an everlasting love. Sometimes, however, that isn't clear to us. And so we get busy and stay that way.

But excessive busyness prevents us from hearing His still, small voice because, well, we're too busy to slow down and actually listen. Busyness equals distraction, and a distracted mind has no room to accommodate anything but its own endless lists, goals, and thoughts.

Yet the Lord's gentle voice invites us to a place of peace—a place where we can actually hear Him. The psalmist says, "He makes me lie down in [fresh, tender] green pastures; He leads me beside the still and restful waters" (Psalm 23:2 AMPC).

Can't you just picture a lovely, gently flowing river surrounded by lush, gradually sloping green banks? Weeping willows and stately oaks accommodate a cozy hammock with your name on it. It's just you, the hammock, a sweet breeze, and the soft whisper of His voice.

Why do we resist going there?

We all have to-do lists and the goal to accomplish everything on them. But when we ceaselessly bow to the pressure of the never-ending list, we live under the tyranny of its demands instead of beside the still, restful waters of His presence, where our true sense of worth can actually be discovered and relished.

Busy Martha's wise sister, Mary, no doubt had such a list (what woman doesn't?) and yet she chose to sit at Jesus's feet anyway. Jesus commended her choice and added that all of the benefits Mary gained from her wise choice would remain with her. "There is only one thing worth being concerned about," Jesus said. "Mary has discovered it, and it will not be taken away from her" (Luke 10:42).

When is the last time we tossed our to-do list aside and simply sat with Jesus? Why do we embrace the tyranny of a never-ending to-do list instead of embracing the One through Whom our truest sense of personal value comes?

> Busyness diminishes us to mere human doings instead of human beings.

Unfortunately, when I was a young girl and before I knew Jesus, my home and heart reverberated with a noise that made it hard to hear His beautiful invitation.

Insignificance on a Whole 'Nother Level

Our entire house pulsated. A cacophony of voices—boisterous laughter, piercing shouts, and overly loud conversations—competed with the rotating Steppenwolf record album that blared all the way down the hall and into my tiny bedroom, daring us kids to try to fall asleep. I shifted in my upper bunk, alternately trembling and angry. My four siblings and I were in bed for the night in theory, but our parents' wild and crazy party was just getting started.

The pungent smell of marijuana drifted under my closed bedroom door, and my heart thumped in my ears. Peering down into the bottom bunk, I saw that my little sister was asleep, though I had no idea how she managed that. I wondered if my three brothers were still awake in their room further down the hall, and if they were as scared as I felt.

As more people showed up, the music volume increased, and my insides quivered. I hated the noise and the raucous atmosphere, but mostly I hated feeling like we kids didn't matter. Like I didn't matter.

Inherently, I knew a wild, blowout party with children at home just wasn't safe. Or right.

Finally, after much tossing and turning, I'd had it. Sleep was not remotely possible. I climbed down the narrow wooden bunk bed ladder, marched my ten-year-old self down the hall toward the family room filled with stoned strangers, and stood there for a moment, trying to locate my mom. When I spotted her, I dug my hands into my skinny little hips and shouted as loud as I could. "Turn down the music!" Then, hot faced, I raced back toward my bunk and, as the party continued, spent the next couple of hours crying into my pillow, wishing everyone would just leave.

That night, and many other similar events in my young life, cumulatively shouted to me what no person needed to speak aloud: *You are insignificant. Your needs, your concerns, your fears, and your desires don't matter. You are too unimportant to be worth consideration.*

As an adult, I have come to realize that injustice fosters insignificance. And few of us get through life without experiencing some form or level of injustice. Nothing makes us feel less significant than when we don't feel heard; when our hearts and desires and even our most basic needs feel disregarded, disrespected, and dismissed.

What a contrasting relief it was to discover the stunning, beautiful truth that God always hears us, He knows our thoughts and hearts, and He values every part of us: our needs, our concerns, our fears, our deepest desires. The psalmist prays, "O LORD, you have examined my heart and know everything about me. You know when I sit down or stand up. You know my thoughts even when I'm far away" (Psalm 139:1-2).

This psalm proclaims a fact our small-feeling hearts desperately need: We are heard, we are seen, we are noticed, and we are *known*.

The Lord knows our very thoughts, so He never misunderstands us. He gets us completely because He made us. Our Creator doesn't scratch His head trying to figure us out—He formed us (Psalm 139:13). The mere idea of being known and intrinsically, accurately understood imparted such a deep relief and joy to my heart that when God first allowed me to fully understand this verse, I sobbed.

That God knows us and understands us communicates how much we matter to Him. It demonstrates our high level of worth in His sight. And it floods our hearts with the beautiful awareness that we are deeply, pricelessly significant to Him.

Not only that, the Lord Himself is our advocate. As the apostle John wrote to the church at Ephesus, "My dear children, I am writing this to you so that you will not sin. But if anyone does sin, *we have an advocate* who pleads our case before the Father. He is Jesus Christ, the one who is truly righteous" (1 John 2:1, italics mine).

Jesus stands up for us. He is our Champion who rescues us, and ultimately, He makes things right.

As in my case, sometimes our inner default is inaccurately set early on, though certainly this can occur at any point in our lives. So when we attempt to understand who we are in Christ, and we're fractured on the inside, we can lack a normal, healthy, God-given sense of significance that most people possess and take for granted.

But as I've learned, when we feel broken, worthless, and insignificant, Jesus takes the initiative and reaches out to us.

A Holy Conversation

Life usually doesn't turn out at all the way we planned, and the subsequent hurts and disappointments can leave a serious dent in our sense of significance. I think this was the case for the unnamed woman in Samaria.

When Jesus and His disciples rolled into town, everyone headed off to find food except for Jesus. Scripture says that in great weariness He sat at the town's well (John 4:6), but He also had a divine appointment.

When this certain Samaritan woman arrived at the well, Jesus wasted no time. He asked for a drink, which astounded her. In fact, she questioned the Lord. Glancing around, she lowered her voice, then dared to ask Him, "Why are *you* talking to *me*?" She knew the routine. Not only did Jewish men avoid speaking to women in public, Jews didn't speak to the despised Samaritans at *all*.

On top of that, this woman wasn't exactly the town's glowing example of noble citizenship. It's doubtful this dear woman grew up thinking she would marry multiple men and wind up with a tarnished reputation. Scripture does not disclose the reasons for her multiple marriages and relationships, but there she was, fetching water midday to avoid the haughty stares and unkind whispers that would otherwise be directed toward her—a disreputable woman.

Yet there Jesus sat, leaning in, speaking to her, and asking for a drink of water, of all things. And their holy conversation was just getting started. But Jesus didn't exactly answer her question. His words to her were more of a divine introduction: "If you only knew the gift God has for you and who you are speaking to, you would ask me, and I would give you living water" (John 4:10).

If you only knew.

What a compelling statement. If we only knew even the smallest fraction of all that He is, of all that He has for us, of all that He thinks of us.

If you only knew.

He speaks these same words to us today. His words reverberate in my heart and, in fact, throughout the earth. Jesus leans in, inviting us to draw near and converse with Him. He longs for us to truly *know Him.* Because He values us. He desires us. He relinquished His very life for us, and He won't be satisfied until He not only captures our hearts, but we know how extraordinary we are to Him.

If we only knew the depth of His love. The depths to which we are known. The depths to which He went to secure a safe, beautiful, eternal place for us. With Him. If we only knew how highly He thinks of us. He treasures us. He gave everything to stand in the gap, to make a way for us to be with Him both here on earth and in eternity.

Jesus knows us. He knows our hearts, our pasts, our conflicts, and our dreams. He knows what we think of ourselves, and He reaches out to let us know that in spite of our pasts—our issues, our tragic mistakes, and the fact that portions of our lives (or maybe our entire lives) have not turned out at all in the way we had hoped—we are important and eternally significant to Him.

He leans in toward our hearts, offering vibrant, living water that satisfies and quenches our deepest unmet needs. He says, "Those who drink the water I give will never be thirsty again. It becomes a fresh, bubbling spring within them, giving them eternal life" (John 4:14).

As their conversation continued, Jesus grew more deliberate. His words touched a place deep within the Samaritan woman's heart, and this precious woman professed a desire for the water Jesus offered her (verse 15).

The dialogue took an unexpected turn when Jesus asked her to go and get her husband. He calmly awaited her response. The Samaritan woman bravely looked into the eyes of love and made a scandalous confession.

> "I don't have a husband," the woman replied. Jesus said, "You're right! You don't have a husband— for you have had five husbands, and you aren't even married to the man you're living with now. You certainly spoke the truth!" (John 4:17).

She let down her guard and allowed herself to be real with Jesus. She dared to look Him in the eye and lay it all out. It's what the Lord desires from us as well. He already knows the truth, yet He waits for us to confess it to Him.

Jesus called her out, but in a way that actually drew her in. He took time to meet with her—not when she had gotten her life together, but right when she needed Him. After all, as He told the Pharisees, "Healthy people don't need a doctor—sick people do. I have come to call not those who think they are righteous, but those who know they are sinners" (Mark 2:17). The Samaritan woman had no illusions about who she was. And that was part of the problem. Yet she was beginning to grasp the identity of the One speaking to her.

Startlingly straightforward, Jesus revealed how intimately He *already* knew her, yet there was no accusation. He affirmed her honesty, and He didn't shun her. This changed everything. He accurately told the Samaritan woman everything she ever did, yet He spoke the truth in love. This precious woman understood that she was known, yet not only did Jesus not judge her, He did not condemn her, and He didn't even tell her to get her act together.

Instead, He reached out to her, offering to meet her deepest need.

As they continued talking, Jesus did something unusual. The One who typically spoke in parables uttered the truth without cloaking it in a story. I believe He did this because He saw that her heart desired the truth, because she was utterly transparent and open with Him, but mostly because He wanted her to know how valuable she was in His eyes. He told her, "I AM the Messiah!" (verse 26).

And she believed Him.

Though the woman from Samaria was nothing short of a hot mess, her heart was drawn to this Man who knew her and whose kind words and actions reflected what He thought of her—that she was precious and significant in His sight.

It was an irresistible encounter.

Jesus went against the cultural norms of the day, astonishing even His disciples (verse 27) in order to reveal two things to the Samaritan woman: His unfailing love and her great worth.

Because the Messiah reached out to her, she began to see herself in a different light. A holy transformation was already starting. She understood that what Jesus offered her was the very thing she had been searching for all of her life. None of her marriages or relationships had ever touched this deep need within her. She not only recognized that Jesus was who He said He was, she embraced the Truth, and she ran with it.

Even when we don't hold a very high opinion of ourselves, Jesus does. He looks beyond our greatest failures and sees our deepest needs. Our past, our mistakes, what others think, and even how we feel about ourselves never lessen our intrinsic value in His eyes. All the things we've walked through—that make us feel less-than, that take a toll and tarnish our hearts and make us doubt our worth—never alter His opinion of us.

You Are Mine

Our then 19-year-old daughter, Emily, was heading home on a Sunday night. So when she texted me at 10:15 p.m., I felt slightly concerned. *I'm bringing something home, and I don't think you're going to be happy about it.* I hoped she wasn't bringing home a traffic ticket but knew she'd arrive in ten minutes, so I camped out by the front window and watched for her headlights.

When her car pulled into our driveway, I stepped out into the muggy night, wrapping my robe around me. Emily jumped out of the car and started walking toward me, holding what looked like a small pile of laundry in her arms. *What on earth?*

That's when I heard the first raspy meow. I looked down into the oversized, bunched-up hoodie Emily held, and there lay the teeniest, scraggliest, most wide-eyed kitten I'd even seen. The poor, frightened little thing was limp and weak and pitifully hoarse from nonstop meowing.

Emily positively glowed. She had seen the kitten in a gas station plaza as it darted into the bushes, and immediately jumped out of the car to coax it over. Only the kitten wouldn't come to her, so she chased it around a lighted sign set in a hedge and eventually was able to grab it.

I shook my head. Good grief. Like we needed another animal to feed. But Emily pleaded, my heart melted, and I figured we could at least house the little thing for a day or two before turning it over— hopefully in better condition—to the Humane Society.

My first thought was Emily's dad was not going to be happy about this. My second thought reminded me that we already had a dog *and* a cat, thank you very much. And my third thought brought my hand up in the air like a school-crossing guard in heavy traffic. As we headed toward our front porch, I did an about-face.

"Turn right around and go buy some flea shampoo," I held up my hand in a stop position, interrupting the protest about to emerge on Emily's lips, "or it's not coming into my house." With that, Emily raced off, kitten wrapped securely in her arms. I stepped back into the house to break the news about our surprise furry guest to Keith.

Several flea baths later, we laid the emaciated, limp little kitty on a cozy towel on the bathroom floor. It still had odd white flecks in its fur, which we couldn't figure out. We did our best to feed it, but it was so young and weak that it couldn't drink much. I thought it might not live through the night and told Emily so. Then I laid a hand on its scraggly, furry side and prayed, bracing myself for the strong possibility of bury-ing a kitten in the morning.

Two days later the vet informed us that our 1.3-pound kitty was not a girl, as we had thought, but a boy. Just five days later the little guy had eaten enough that he finally had strength to run through our house for the first time. Emily decided to name him Jaxon, which means "God has been gracious"; clearly, the night Emily found Jaxon, God had indeed been gracious.

Determined to nurse the kitten back to health so he could find a forever home, we made the family decision to keep him for the next few weeks until he was old enough to place for adoption. In the mean-time, we also learned that the odd white flecks in Jaxon's fur were…cat lice. I know. Revolting. I had no idea cat lice even existed, and for the next four weeks I staged an epic battle. Me against enough fleas to cover a brontosaurus and a flat-out battalion of stubborn, impossibly repro-ducing, disgusting kitty lice.

It was way more than I had signed up for. And if I never pick another lice egg out of an animal's fur again, I will do a handspring, thank you very much.

We paid for all of Jaxon's shots and other veterinary care, finally bid farewell to the fleas and lice (oh happy day!), and even found a fam-ily who was eager to adopt him. But in the end (you guessed it), we fell hard for little Jaxon and couldn't part with him. As I write this, our furry, adorable, always entertaining little buddy is now one year old—a thriving, sweet, unexpected gift of immense joy.

Recently, Emily told me that keeping Jaxon had been her plan all along. She figured it would take three days; that if he was in our home for three days, her dad and I would be toast.

All I know is my daughter spotted a sick, emaciated little kitten des-perately needing to be rescued, hiding behind a gas station sign, and her heart could not resist. Apparently, neither could ours. Within just a few weeks, we knew that we were Jaxon's family and our home was his. That bedraggled little kitty belonged to us.

In many ways, I think our various stories match Jaxon's. Though we may not physically be homeless, starving, or covered with parasites (let's just pause right here and utter our solemn gratitude), our struggles and experiences make us feel too small and unimportant to be what we might consider worthy of consideration. So we languish on the inside and hide away.

But God sees us and has pity on us. He pursues us and goes after us—His heart cannot resist. He reaches out and speaks softly to us, drawing us close to Him, winning our trust and capturing our hearts. When the time is right, He gently begins removing the heart crud that is sucking away our very lives. He does this because we are His, and He could no more resist helping us than Emily could resist rescuing Jaxon that late summer night. We belong to Him.

The Lord also begins and takes great pleasure in the process of making our hearts radiant and beautiful. The psalmist says, "The Lord takes pleasure in His people; He will beautify the humble with salvation and adorn the wretched with victory" (Psalm 149:4 AMPC).

If anyone was ever wretched, it was me. Maybe you can relate. And maybe you can rejoice with me, because as we humble ourselves in His presence, He makes us beautiful. He makes all things beautiful in their time, including us (Ecclesiastes 3:11).

Being made beautiful is a holy process. We don't always perceive what God is doing deep within us. Ultimately, we must choose to surrender and entrust ourselves to His tender, loving care—even the uncomfortable parts, when He handpicks off the stuff clinging to our hearts.

A Glorious New Wardrobe

I'm not a shopper. It's shocking, I know. Most women adore shopping. I endure it. Which explains my wardrobe. Most of my clothes are functional, practical, and durable. Hardly the stuff of high fashion, much to my occasional dismay. Like when I show up at an event and everyone looks so beautifully pulled together and coordinated and flowy. It's then that I long for a savvy personal fashionista shopper who knows my size and colors. Or even just the time and desire to invest in giving my wardrobe more pizzazz (Is *pizzazz* even a hip clothing word? Probably not. *Sigh.*).

When I first read the following Scripture verse, I pictured a lovely woman with flowing, shiny hair blowing in the wind, wearing a sparkling, ethereal gown. The kind I'd love to wear if I was ever invited somewhere one wears such things.

> The King's daughter in the inner part [of the palace] is all glorious; her clothing is inwrought with gold (Psalm 45:13 AMPC).

Though I've not yet received an invitation that requires a shimmering ball gown (but you never know!), I have been invited into the inner part of the King's palace, and so have you.

It's the inner place where He transforms us into what He always intended before the enemy wreaked havoc, before we were pummeled and stripped of our dignity. The inner palace is a place of sacred privilege, where our very essence is understood and intensely valued and healed. It's the place of intimacy with Jesus—the place where He adorns us in holy elegance and a glorious and lovely heart.

Gold speaks of the incorruptible nature with which He clothes us. Gold is an exceedingly durable element that resists all corrosion. It doesn't tarnish or rust. In fact, there is no natural substance currently known that can destroy gold. And so when we remain in Christ, the beautiful work He accomplishes on the inside—the inward adornment we allow Him to accomplish and strive to retain—is incorruptible and unfading (1 Peter 3:4).

We are covered in exquisite, incorruptible clothing that shimmers with His radiance. This expresses the eternal, lasting quality of healing and change the Lord alone can accomplish in us. He redeems our pain and makes us beautiful inside and out, crowning us with love and mercy and dignity (Psalm 103:4). Because we are His. Because we matter, and in His sight we are captivating.

As He continues working in our hearts and our very souls, He brushes aside our despair and adorns us with a crown of beauty. He converts our grief into sparkling joy. As the prophet Isaiah promised, "To all who mourn in Israel, he will give a crown of beauty for ashes, a joyous blessing instead of mourning, festive praise instead of despair. In their righteousness, they will be like great oaks that the LORD has planted for his own glory" (Isaiah 61:3).

In Him we are stable. Beautiful. Important. Significant. It's in Him that we are all glorious. It's how He sees us. He brings us into His presence, changes the wardrobe of our souls, and we are transformed.

It's then that we realize we are not important because of what we do but because of Whose we are. Our heavenly Father cherishes us and crowns us with honor, and it's a crown that never slips off, even when harsh circumstances crash right into our hearts. The psalmist asked:

> What are mere mortals that you should think about them, human beings that you should care for them? Yet you made them only a little lower than God and crowned them with glory and honor (Psalm 8:4-5).

Yes, we are mere mortals. Yes, our sense of significance can be seriously dented by others. Yes, sometimes we mistakenly allow others to gauge our significance. But why would we settle for any of that when we are *His*? He beams as He watches over us because He loves us. His glory and honor rest on us.

- When the world says we don't matter, God says we are precious in His sight, and He loves us (Isaiah 43:4).

- When our past shrieks that we are worthless, God says we are cleansed, made holy, and made right with Him by calling on Christ (1 Corinthians 6:11).

- When our circumstances scream we don't matter, God reminds us that although we may be pressed on every side, we are not crushed; though we are perplexed, we are not driven to despair; and even when we are hunted down, we are never abandoned by Him (2 Corinthians 4:8).

- When others treat us as if we don't matter, God says He will surely be gracious to us at the sound of our cry, and when He hears us, He will answer (Isaiah 30:19).

- When our consciences accuse us, God sprinkles our consciences with Christ's blood to make us clean, and He washes us with pure water (Hebrews 10:22).

- When seemingly unanswered prayers imply we don't matter, God assures us that His plans stand firm forever (Psalm 33:11), and that His plans for us are good (Jeremiah 29:11).

Because He so deeply loves and values us, our God of justice offers us His love, peace, favor, joy, and victory, but even more—He offers us "His matchless, unbroken companionship" (Isaiah 30:18 AMPC).

And His matchless, unbroken companionship changes everything.

Knowing Whose we are enables us to embrace our own healthy sense of significance, while treating others with that same sense of worth. Ironically, when we dare to believe we are significant, we will lead lives of great significance.

> He beams as He watches over us because He loves us.

May God, Who is kind and gracious, remove from our hearts every seed of insignificance planted by the enemy. And may He, in His great goodness, replace every one with divine seeds of significance until our hearts brim with the resounding truth that yes, we are significant. Because in His sight, every iota of us matters.

Your Personal Proclamation:
SAY IT. KNOW IT. BELIEVE IT.

God sees me through eyes of love, and His heart says to mine *You are Mine. You matter. You are significant.* And I believe Him. I will not garner my significance from the things I do, but from the One I belong to. I am chosen, known, precious, honored, and deeply and accurately understood and valued by Him. I matter. My thoughts and ideas and opinions matter, and what concerns me concerns the Lord.

God so greatly values me that He offers me His love, joy, peace, and favor—and His matchless, unbroken companionship. He holds a high opinion of me and sees beyond my greatest failures and counts me as significant anyway. I am cherished and adorned in holy elegance. I am being clothed with a gloriously healed and lovely heart. I am significant.

8

It Shatters the Bleakest Despair

I WILL GIVE YOU HOPE

The Scripture says, No man who believes in Him
[who adheres to, relies on, and trusts in Him] will
[ever] be put to shame or be disappointed.

ROMANS 10:11 AMPC

It landed on us like a stealth hand grenade. Shock and awe boomer-anged between my husband and me, and as we initially processed the devastating news, anguish settled into our hearts like so much lethal shrapnel. We were in a major family crisis, and as I slogged through those first painful days, I couldn't help but think that the awful mess unfolding was the exact opposite of everything I'd ever prayed or hoped for. The opposite of all I yearned to see.

As my husband wrestled with anger toward God, I struggled against an emotional tsunami that knocked my feet out from under me. My heart literally throbbed. For days I carried a thick washcloth around the house with me to absorb the constant flow of tears over which I had no control. Desperate for serenity, I downed chamomile tea like a British dame, and every single breath was an anguished prayer.

I did not want to be here in this raw, awful place.

I stared out the window and watched neighbors chat on the side-walk, kids shout and laugh as their bikes whizzed past our house. The sun rose and set, and our pets clamored to be fed. Incomprehensibly, life kept moving forward. I knew I should fight the inward spiral, but frankly, I couldn't. My brain couldn't even formulate cohesive thoughts. My heart felt completely overwhelmed. Despondent. Panicky.

Sometimes we have to face circumstances we never imagined—events that not only hit us hard, but attempt to lead us by the hand straight into the arms of despair.

It's what happened to Jesus's disciples.

I think hindsight prevents us from fully understanding the absolute devastation Jesus's followers experienced following His crucifixion. More than 2000 years later, we benefit by reading about it from the vantage point of knowing exactly how it all turned out. But Jesus's followers walked through the soul-darkening, devastating reality of—and what they most certainly considered the brutal tragedy of—His death, without fully comprehending what was happening.

Their beloved Friend—the One who had performed glorious miracle after miracle, the One who stilled the wind and the waves, the One that Peter declared to be the Messiah—was put to death by Roman soldiers. And it seemed to His followers that their hopes had been put to death as well. Not one of them understood why everything they had prayed and hoped for had apparently come to nothing.

I imagine a stunned silence resonating in Jerusalem and the surrounding area during those initial hours after Jesus's horrific torture and crucifixion. Shock waves reverberated in every heart. Chores were done on tiptoe, and silence dominated as every believer struggled to process what had just happened.

An unexpected, scary reality had swept in like a tidal wave, making a mess of the disciples' hopes and beliefs plunging them into deep confusion, and sweeping them toward the cliff of despair. Not a single one of them wanted to be in such a raw, awful place.

The Exact Opposite of What We Hoped For

As my husband and I adjusted to our scary new reality, I fought discouragement and fear—a lethal combination. Though I had seen God answer prayer—I was a praying woman, after all—and I continued praying like crazy, it seemed like the reality we were facing trumped everything else.

Have you been there? Are you facing a harsh reality that appears to overturn and dominate everything else?

All the things the disciples had seen Jesus do—the healings, the miracles, even defying the laws of gravity and nature—what did they now mean? All their subsequent convictions, beliefs, hopes, and thoughts led them to believe one thing, and now the exact opposite had happened. The One they thought had come to rescue the entire earth had died in a gruesome way that none of them could stop, seemingly bringing all their hopes to a tragic end.

Jesus was dead. Had they been misled?

But a powerful principle was at work. One Jesus Himself had explained to them.

> I assure you, most solemnly I tell you, unless a grain of wheat falls into the earth and dies, it remains [just one grain; it never becomes more but lives] by itself alone. But if it dies, it produces many others and yields a rich harvest (John 12:24 AMPC).

What if when our hopes come to nothing and appear to die, God is really at work, in spite of how things appear—in spite of our confusion, disappointment, and heartache? Could it be our hopes are then sown in order to produce much more hope and yield a rich harvest of promise?

If there is one thing our current heart-crippling event was teaching me, it's that our hope cannot depend upon perfect, well-turned-out circumstances. Our hope is Jesus walking with us down that confusing, grief-laden road.

How many times does it appear that our hopes have come to nothing? How many times do we stumble down the road, wondering where on earth Jesus could be in all the mess? How many times do we allow the reality of the circumstances to override God's truth and the very promise He has graciously slipped into our hearts?

After the (to all appearances) shocking tragedy of the crucifixion, two of Jesus's followers walked along the road to Emmaus, talking and trying to make sense of it all. In an astonishing, unexpected turn of events, Jesus appeared and began walking with them.

But they didn't recognize Him.

In their grief, the disciples walking that road didn't even recognize Jesus (see Luke 24:13-16). Don't we sometimes do the same thing? Does the overwhelming pain of our circumstances prevent us from recognizing Jesus right beside us?.

Later, after arriving at their destination, they convinced Jesus to eat with them. As soon as Jesus broke the bread, their eyes were opened. And at that very moment, Jesus disappeared (Luke 24:28-31). It was then that His followers realized Jesus had been with them all long. "They said to each other, 'Didn't our hearts burn within us as he talked with us on the road and explained the Scriptures to us?'" (Luke 24:32).

What if Jesus is right there with us in the dark places, the scary places, the places we never wanted to glance at, much less experience and deal with? What if we allow Him to open our eyes like He did for those disciples (see Luke 24:30-31) and show us the bigger picture and the hope to which we are called?

What if He allows us to endure the loss of hope so that something even bigger than we hoped for can transpire?

Shake It Off

Like the apostle Paul, I needed to learn—we need to learn—the wisdom of shaking off our odds-defying circumstances. Gale-force winds shipwrecked Paul along with the entire ship's crew and passengers on the island of Malta. Locals met them on the beach, bringing blankets as Paul and his shipmates helped light fires to warm up and dry off. Then something devastating happened.

> As Paul gathered an armful of sticks and was laying them on the fire, a poisonous snake, driven out by the heat, bit him on the hand. The people of the island saw it hanging from his hand and said to each other, "A murderer, no

doubt! Though he escaped the sea, justice will not permit him to live." But Paul shook off the snake into the fire and was unharmed (Acts 28:3-5).

The Amplified Version of this verse identifies the snake as a viper. Yet though Paul was indeed bitten, and a viper has seriously long fangs that inject deadly venom, he merely shook off the snake and suffered no ill effects whatsoever.

What an astonishing reaction.

I would have screamed, sobbed, and shown the entire crowd the bite marks. Of all the possible reactions I can imagine, simply shaking the snake off into the fire and going about my business is probably the last thing I would have done.

A snakebite punctures the skin, injecting poisonous venom with lethal properties designed to immobilize the prey. But Paul didn't freak out. It's almost like he expected the bite and assumed that God would protect him. Paul's reaction to the snake—and the fact that it did not kill him—was an incredible testimony to the natives of Malta, who had expected him to die.

I love how Paul merely shook the snake off of his hand, paying little attention, and expecting no negative consequences. It's an excellent goal for us as well.

Paul responded in mind-boggling faith—a faith to which I unashamedly aspire—by not allowing the snakebite to impede him. He wasn't about to allow it to hamper his goal or harm him or dim his hopes on what lay before him.

What if when venomous things such as accusations, devastating news, or tragic circumstances strike at us, we likewise simply shook them off? We could, instead of staring at and reflecting on the situation, decide to let it go. What if the venomous strike of the enemy was unable to immobilize our hope?

Offenses will come. Hurts will happen. Disappointments, irritations, and completely unfair things wait ahead for us all. There will be many, many times when we must deal with issues. Through prayer, God gives us wisdom and discernment to know when to speak the truth in love (Ephesians 4:15), but even then, the results are out of our hands. Sometimes there will be situations where we just simply do our best and then, like Paul, we must shake them off.

Shaking them off will require forgiveness and positive, Scripture-based self-talk, plus the willingness to believe and trust that God is in the middle of all that's happening.

What if we hoped for and expected God to move in our circumstances instead of assuming the worst? Instead of expecting the venom to take hold?

When we shake off the enemy's worst intentions and keep our expectations in the One who is able to fulfill His promises to us, hope can bubble to the surface of our hearts.

And that's exactly what we need when we're headed into unknown territory.

Navigating the Uncharted

After the stealth hand grenade hit our family, it became clear God was calling my husband and me to walk out a new level of faith. He desired for us to trust Him to a degree we couldn't fathom, and I confess my faith fell far, far short. I wrestled with truly trusting God, with knowing His strong hand was on our situation, especially when it appeared hopeless. I struggled to hold on to hope.

How *do* we hold on to hope when our feet are knocked out from under us? When the focus of our hope has died? When nothing has turned out as we had hoped?

As wise women we must recognize that our hope cannot remain intact when its very infrastructure is built around any particular set of circumstances or outcomes. Because all that means is we have hope as long as things go according to our plans. And when the circumstances fall apart, our hope will evaporate. I think to a degree many of us unwittingly do this. And we don't recognize it until the thing upon which we had pinned our hopes doesn't work out at all the way we imagined.

As the disciples soon discovered, God's ways don't come close to resembling our ways.

"My thoughts are nothing like your thoughts," says the LORD. "And my ways are far beyond anything you could imagine. For just as the heavens are higher than the earth, so my ways are higher than your ways and my thoughts higher than your thoughts" (Isaiah 55:8-9).

Hope—genuine, radiant, unfaltering hope that doesn't evaporate in the scorching heat of adverse conditions—is inextricably entwined with faith and trust. And the recipient upon which we pin our faith and our trust can never be anything less than the One who is worthy and able and utterly trustworthy.

How do we maintain our hope while navigating the sometimes harsh reality of our circumstances? When circumstances threaten to make a mess of our hope, we must plunge our stake of faith-filled trust into the Solid Rock. Jesus. He alone has the ability to anchor us to hope. In fact, He *is* our hope. Even when we don't see the very thing we long to see.

One of the most powerful things hope does is help us to accept reality without crumbling. Like Abraham, we can face facts without wavering.

And Abraham's faith did not weaken, even though, at about 100 years of age, he figured his body was as good as dead—and so was Sarah's womb. Abraham never wavered in believing God's promise. In fact, his faith grew stronger, and in this he brought glory to God. He was fully convinced that God is able to do whatever he promises (Romans 4:19-21).

Abraham was an old man with a barren wife, yet he trusted God over mere facts. We, too, can navigate hopeless-looking situations, believing—being fully persuaded as Abraham was—that God has the power to do what He promised us.

But if we want to get to the place where hope is deeply embedded in our hearts, we must be willing to diligently cultivate it. Hope doesn't mysteriously appear but must be deliberately developed. It takes root and develops as we study God's Word, witnessing His faithfulness through the eyes of those who've gone before us. And we must choose to trust God (and keep trusting Him!) in spite of how things appear. It requires diligence, faith, and persistence, particularly where our minds are concerned

Abraham is called the father of our faith because he showed us the way by holding on to hope even when his answer was delayed for 25 years. He demonstrated by example how to walk in faith and continue believing, even when his dream of having a child seemed unattainable because his body was as good as dead.

A Fresh, New Default Setting

Hope must become our default setting, so that no matter what situational grenade drops on us, our hope is still intact. How? By practicing.

The author of Hebrews says that practicing hope prevents us from becoming spiritual sluggards—those who don't inherit the promises God offers. As we press on in faith, daring to believe all of God's promises, we're actually practicing hope!

> In order that you may not grow disinterested and become [spiritual] sluggards, but imitators, behaving as do those who through faith (by their leaning of the entire personality on God in Christ in absolute trust and confidence in His power, wisdom, and goodness) *and by practice of patient endurance and waiting* are [now] inheriting the promises (Hebrews 6:12 AMPC, italics mine).

Practice involves enduring and waiting—not my favorite things. But through these, our faith and hope grow. We must practice faith and hope over and over. Even when our situations have us feeling like a hot mess. Especially when we're reduced to a hot mess.

As we continue to practice and grow our hope, it will solidify and become an anchor for our hearts. Hope will anchor us firmly in the place of peace and prevent us from holding hands with despair.

> God has given both his promise and his oath. These two

> things are unchangeable because it is impossible for God to
> lie. Therefore, we who have fled to him for refuge can have
> great confidence as we hold to the hope that lies before us.
> This hope is a strong and trustworthy anchor for our souls.
> It leads us through the curtain into God's inner sanctuary
> (Hebrews 6:18-19).

Hope lies before us. Always. It is strong and trustworthy and anchors us as we choose—in the midst of all that would rip hope right out of our hearts—to practice it over and over. This is how hope becomes our default setting.

As the days and weeks passed, it sometimes felt like Keith and I were living a surreal "Twilight Zone" episode. But I decided to dare to hope anyway. To hope and believe that in spite of how devastating things appeared, God would be able to accomplish His will and plans and purpose anyway. That He would hear my prayers and use them to change things.

Isn't that the whole point of hope? To buoy our hearts so that when the overwhelming hits, we don't throw up a white flag and flat give up? To give us holy perspective that enables us to stand and pray, and that puts everything else in its place?

Obviously, this was the path God had us on for now, and though I didn't like it, I didn't want to let go of hope. In fact, I refused. I anchored myself to God's hope. It was the anchor my heart and soul desperately needed.

Tiptoeing Forward with Our Eyes Closed

Abraham knew a thing or two about hope. God told him to pack up and move, and though it wasn't in Abraham's plans, he did. And the flabbergasting part is even though God didn't show him where, exactly, he was going, Abraham didn't worry about it. He just obeyed and moved forward one step at a time.

How? How did Abraham obey, leave his homeland, and head to who knows where without worrying?

By faith. Pure, simple, radical faith. And we cannot maintain hope without vibrant faith—faith that compels us to believe God whatever the cost.

Abraham completely, radically trusted and hoped in his God. Do we? Do our responses and actions back up our words? When was the last time God gave us radical marching orders, and we simply nodded in agreement and pursued that very thing? And why do our brains instantly—instantly!—switch into stress-out, figure-out mode?

> [Urged on] by faith Abraham, when he was called, obeyed and went forth to a place which he was destined to receive as an inheritance; and he went, although he did not know or trouble his mind about where he was to go. [Prompted] by faith he dwelt as a temporary resident in the land which was designated in the promise [of God, though he was like a stranger] in a strange country, living in tents with Isaac and Jacob, fellow heirs with him of the same promise. For he was [waiting expectantly and confidently] looking forward to the city which has fixed and firm foundations, whose Architect and Builder is God (Hebrews 11:8-10 AMPC).

Does the Lord have that freedom with us? Does Almighty God, the Architect and Builder of our very lives, have this outrageous level of freedom in our lives? Are we willing to accommodate and obey Him, even when we're uncertain where all this is leading us?

Velcro Hearts

I didn't yet want a grenade-level family crisis. However, I chose to believe that our shrapnel-ridden situation was not bigger than my God. Part of that meant learning to recognize and resist the enemy's lies.

Sometimes we succumb to his deceptions. It's one of the ways he extinguishes our hope—by whispering plausible falsehoods that line up with the current facts we're facing and squelch every trace of beautiful hope within us.

But distinguishing truth from lies enables us to reject the enemy's lies, cling to God's truth and His promises, and retain our hope. When

I sense myself coming into agreement with distress, confusion, or fear concerning a situation I'm facing, it's a sure sign I'm listening to a lie. I take notice. Then I take action: I pray.

We must ask the Lord to grant us discernment and to enable us to hear our tender Shepherd's voice over the resounding lies of our adversary. Prayer enables us to accurately discern God's soft whisper, shutting out the enemy's lies.

Prayer should be instinctive, like gulping air after emerging from underwater. If prayer is not instinctive for you, ask God to help you to pray more and pray first. He will. Ask Him to increase your discernment so that you will recognize the enemy's lies and resist them, while recognizing the Lord's still, small voice and embracing it instead.

Because embracing His voice Velcros hope to our hearts.

A Hope Detour

My friend Angela and I were visiting Tampa for a long overdue girlfriend weekend to see Beth Moore in person at the Sun Dome. Neither of us had ever seen Beth live, and we were excited and expectant. What a joy. At the end of the event's first evening, as the worship team sang the final song, we hurried out to my car to beat the mad rush of 7000 other women.

Since I had previously lived in the area, I knew exactly where I needed to go in order to jump back onto the interstate and get us back to our hotel in the most efficient manner. Backing out of the parking space, I steered my car in the direction I needed to go, but bright orange cones and a parking attendant blocked me. Frustrated, I sucked in my breath and tried to find a way to drive to where I needed to go. I ended up flipping a U further down the road so I could get back to where I had been, and then we squirted out onto the main road that led to Interstate 75.

No such luck the next day. When the Saturday session ended just after noon, though, I had a different agenda. Angela and I had plans to remain in Tampa to hit a local bakery and then eat lunch. Again, I knew exactly where I needed to go. And the funny thing is, the road I needed to access was literally right in front of us. But this time half of the Tampa police force was on the scene, blocking every single road pointed in the direction I needed to go.

I could not get to that road.

Sucking in another deep breath of frustration, I groaned. I was being rerouted exactly where I didn't need to go. All the traffic was forced to flow in one direction, which happened to be in the opposite direction of where I was headed. Every single turn was blocked. I wanted to scream. (I know, you'd think after a Beth Moore conference I'd be wearing a halo and passing out cold water bottles to all the police officers.) Irritated, I groaned and complained to my friend as I drove in the wrong direction, wondering why on earth my car was being routed where I did not need to go, and wondering how long it would take me to get back to where I needed to be.

After about five minutes of reluctantly driving the wrong way (with lots of spitting and popping on my part), we arrived at a stoplight I did not recognize. Completely discombobulated, I didn't know what cross street we were at. On a whim, I turned left and then finally saw a street sign. I recognized the name but realized this was a new road extension that had not existed back when I lived in Tampa. Consequently, I still couldn't figure out exactly where we were.

We soon reached another traffic light, and as it turned red and I brought my car to a stop, my eyebrows rose. I realized I was at the precise cross streets I had hoped to get to. Somehow, in spite of *not* going in the direction I *knew* I needed to go, I wound up exactly where I needed to be.

It made absolutely no sense. And yet here we were, only two minutes from the finest gluten-free bakery on the planet.

Sometimes the way that seems wrong—our hard circumstances, the unfair situation, the shrapnel of pain exploding in our hearts—is steering us in a way we would never choose to go. Never. And sometimes it is a way we believe couldn't possibly be right because *we know* the correct direction we should be going. And this way—this blocked-off, makes-no-sense way—seems to us utterly, completely wrong.

But what if we dared to believe that in the midst of our mess, God is actually in control? That He is sovereign? That He knows best, and

He is ultimately steering things and leading us exactly where we need to be—even if it is in a new direction that makes no sense? Will we yield to His way? Will we trust Him to make a way?

> Behold, I am doing a new thing! Now it springs forth; do you not perceive and know it and will you not give heed to it? I will even make a way in the wilderness and rivers in the desert (Isaiah 43:19 AMPC).

After the crucifixion, Jesus's disciples took a hope detour. Clearly, I did as well. I think every one of has taken a hope detour at some point in our lives—sometimes many, many times.

Ultimately, however, what looked like the wrong way turned out to be the right way. God's way. The victorious way. It just took His followers (and me!) some time to figure it all out.

At the beginning of the chapter, I shared about a family crisis that knocked us for a loop. And though I cannot downplay the emotional toll it took on us, I can say this: God has used it in a way I never imagined. He enabled me to hold on to hope through it all, and He will do the same for you.

Elisabeth Elliot said, "Sometimes the worst has to happen in order for the best to happen. We hold a high hope, we lose it, and to our utter surprise something infinitely better than we had hoped is given to us."

Jesus's entire life looked nothing like anyone expected. His birth and His death left many flummoxed. But it all ultimately unfolded exactly as God would have it. But Jesus entrusted Himself to His Father, knowing that God's ultimate plan and purpose would prevail, and something infinitely better would unfold.

Should we do any less?

Should we not entrust ourselves—every aspect of our lives—to our heavenly Father, trusting that God's ultimate plan and purpose will prevail? What if we dared to release our limited hopes (limited in

Prayer should be instinctive, like gulping air after emerging from underwater.

God's perspective) and instead believed that something infinitely better will unfold?

What if, like Abraham, we journey toward the unknown and through the sometimes excruciating difficulties and sacrifices without losing hope? What if we don't allow detours to rattle us, trusting that God will get us exactly where we need to be in His perfect timing?

What if our apparent loss of hope—the death of the very thing we prayed and stood and believed for—is actually the birth of something far more beautiful? Something bigger and better than we imagined?

> Our light, momentary affliction (this slight distress of the passing hour) is ever more and more abundantly preparing and producing and achieving for us an everlasting weight of glory [beyond all measure, excessively surpassing all comparisons and all calculations, a vast and transcendent glory and blessedness never to cease!]. Since we consider and look not to the things that are seen but to the things that are unseen; for the things that are visible are temporal (brief and fleeting), but the things that are invisible are deathless and everlasting (2 Corinthians 4:17-18 AMPC).

God is declaring through this passage—one of the most powerful in all of Scripture—that the afflictions we are enduring (which Paul declares are light and momentary, though they feel heavy and oppressive and nearly unbearable here and now) are actually accomplishing something beautiful and eternal in us and for us. They are producing an incalculable glory that will never cease.

It's *not* all for nothing. There *is* a beautiful, glorious point to it all. There is hope.

That means that the awful tragedies we endure, the disappointing heartbreak God allows, the pain of circumstances we feel powerless against are accomplishing deep and permanent and glorious change in us and glory and honor for Him.

Our circumstances, however arduous, are temporary. Our destiny and our future are not. And there is an incomparable future glory that surpasses everything our mind can conjure.

That is the hope God offers us.

This stunningly beautiful, eternal perspective changes everything. Our hope is in the invisible things—the promises God has whispered to our hearts—and in His triumphant ability to do exceedingly and abundantly beyond all we can dare to hope or imagine.

> May the God of your hope so fill you with all joy and peace
> in believing [through the experience of your faith] that by
> the power of the Holy Spirit you may abound and be over-
> flowing (bubbling over) with hope (Romans 15:13 AMPC).

May the Lord give us hope that bubbles and overflows continually. The hope that no person, no circumstance, and no devil in hell can ever take from us. May He cause our hearts to burn within us as He walks with us and talks with us on our difficult journeys.

God offers us hope in the most unlikely moments, in our darkest despair. His hope lifts our hearts. It tells us things can change—that we can change. Hope whispers that our situation won't always be this way. Like weighty Florida humidity, divine hope hangs in the air, just waiting to be inhaled.

No matter what hits us, we can always have hope.

Fresh, beautiful, real hope.

It's ours.

Your Personal Proclamation:
SAY IT. KNOW IT. BELIEVE IT.

I will not allow myself to become fixated on my current circumstances. I will instead shake off every venomous circumstance that strikes at me, and I will turn my heart toward Jesus. I will hope for and expect the Lord. My hope will not remain on how any particular set of circumstances unfolds, but on the Lord, Who is sovereign, holy, faithful, and trustworthy. I will yield to God's way even when (especially when) I feel I know better, and I will not allow the unexpected course my life is taking to shake me and steal my hope.

I will cultivate and hold on to genuine, radiant, unfaltering hope—the kind that doesn't evaporate in the scorching heat of adversity—until it takes root and develops fully into authentic faith, trust, and hope in Christ alone. My heart will be anchored in Christ and anchored in holy hope.

Neither Our Guilt Complex Nor Our Doubts Nor Our Catastrophic Failures Can Separate Us

I WILL GIVE YOU MY UNFAILING LOVE

I also pray that you will understand the incredible
greatness of God's power for us who believe him.

EPHESIANS 1:19

As a girl, I experienced tangible love mostly in the summertime, which I spent the majority of at the Detroit home of my beloved gram and Boopa (my mangled, baby-talk version of Grampa, which stuck). Huddled among rows of humble, working-class northern bungalow-style houses, a gorgeous sycamore tree crowned my grandparents' front yard, and a sparkling oasis of an above-ground red, white, and blue aluminum swimming pool glimmered in the backyard.

If my family home an hour away was a wasteland of neglect, Gram's home was a haven of comfort and love. A master seamstress, Gram sewed many of her own clothes, suits for Boopa, beautiful curtains for her living room, and even a pair of groovy orange bell-bottoms with a matching top for me. We'd chat together while drinking Faygo red pop with our lunch, and she always let me choose special foods on our weekly trip to Farmer Jack's grocery store (my standard picks? Apple

Jacks and chicken and rice soup). Gram allowed me to invite friends over to swim and eat ground-bologna sandwiches at the wooden picnic table next to the pool. It wasn't fancy, but it felt like paradise, and I always felt cherished, safe, and secure.

In between those oasis periods lurked my real life and serious neglect. Parents not home. Indifference and disinterest (or worse, violent fights) when they were. Three-foot-high piles of dirty clothing overflowing the laundry room until they blocked and overtook the adjacent half bath. Perpetually empty fridge and kitchen cupboards. Zero toilet paper. Anger. Fear. Lots of tears and confusion.

And while I acknowledge the sin nature that dwells in me—in us all—and that even with perfect parents I might have struggled with love (what it means, how it looks, and how to give and receive it), those dark years of my early youth shaped my ideas of life in general and of love in particular.

So when a girl who tragically misunderstands her own value grows into adolescence and then young adulthood, she makes heart-rending choices. Choices that lead her into the eager arms of counterfeit love— the kind that leaves her shaken and insecure—and she drifts further and further from the truth of unfailing love.

And in the fertile ground of an insecure, aching heart, the enemy sows the biggest lie of all: *You aren't loved.* But Satan doesn't stop there. He taunts us, whispering what our deceived hearts already suspect: *No one will ever love you. You're too _____. Who could love you when you_____? And God? He could never love you…He stays far away from people like you.*

We begin to sense that God might love other people—lots of other people—but not us. Our hearts feel doomed, cut off from the love He clearly doles out on those far more worthy.

I might have remained in that isolated place of tormenting accusation—the place where a hot mess like me usually languishes—if not for God's red-hot pursuit of my heart. In spite of my misconceptions, His amazing love was already at work, pursuing me.

> Surely Your goodness and unfailing love will pursue me all the days of my life (Psalm 23:6).

What a stunning thought: *God's love pursues us.* It always has, and it always will. His relentless love compels Him to win our hearts. And He doesn't even wait until we know Him. He yearns for us, paid an unimaginable price for us, and is determined for us to know that we didn't choose Him. *He chose us.*

He pursues us *all* the days of our lives. When we know Him and when we don't. When we're living for Him and when we're not. My mind struggles to grasp this extravagant love. Though I lived under the influence of great darkness with an increasingly distorted concept of love (and the accompanying sinful actions), He pursued me. Scripture reveals that even when I didn't know Him, while I was out in the big ol' world living exactly as I pleased, God's love compelled Him to act on my behalf:

> God—so rich is He in His mercy! Because of and in order to satisfy the great and wonderful and intense love with which He loved us, even when we were dead (slain) by [our own] shortcomings and trespasses, He made us alive together in fellowship and in union with Christ (Ephesians 2:4-5 AMPC).

God desires to satisfy His intense love for us, so He seeks fellowship and union with us. What an awesome demonstration of His wonderful love for me, for you, for us all. While we were dead in our sins— and girl, you'd better believe I was good and dead—He made us alive. He makes all of us alive in Christ. He heaps great grace on us. In spite of our glaring filth, He reaches out. It makes no sense, and yet there it is.

Love compelled God to act. When my children were babies, love compelled me to hold them close, habitually inhale their soft, new-baby scent, and smother them with kisses. It didn't matter if they'd kept me up half the night or spit up on my best shirt—I absolutely had to snuggle them every other moment of the day. I could no more keep them out of my arms (and heart) than a bald-tired clunker can stop on a wet road without skidding. Likewise, God couldn't hold back—it's His very nature because God *is* love (1 John 4:16).

Looking back, I can see God's love at work in me, though I didn't realize it at the time. Many years before our family finally splintered and things got really bad, my parents occasionally attended a local church. At the age of seven, however, I adored church and couldn't bear to miss a single week. So come Sunday I walked to church, often alone, though sometimes I cajoled one of my younger brothers to join me. I sat in the wooden pews, held the hymnal close, and sang every stanza. When the kids were dismissed, I raced down the hall toward Sunday school, eager to soak up the Bible stories. Though I didn't understand and could not have expressed it, God was drawing me even then.

God draws us so that we can begin to understand and even desire His great love. He awakens our hearts to the surprising knowledge that we are desired, cherished, and deeply loved.

Love at Work

Not only does God lavish His love on us, but this mighty love changes everything. How? In many and deep ways, but the primary way His love begins to change us is by softening our hearts. The Lord removes our hearts of stone and replaces them with hearts of flesh, which sounds strange but is actually a beautiful thing. As God spoke through the prophet Ezekiel, "I will give you a new heart, and I will put a new spirit in you. I will take out your stony, stubborn heart and give you a tender, responsive heart" (Ezekiel 36:26).

A hard heart is unyielding, brittle, yet difficult to penetrate, and is concerned primarily with its own self. A hard heart prevents us from believing and trusting God and from entering into all He has for us. It leads us the wrong way every time. The author of Hebrews warns us, pointing out exactly what a hard heart looks like:

> [Beware] brethren, take care, lest there be in any one of you a wicked, unbelieving heart [which refuses to cleave to, trust in, and rely on Him], leading you to turn away and desert or stand aloof from the living God (Hebrews 3:12 AMPC).

Love requires us to believe. But even then softening is not an instantaneous thing. It's more of a slow surrender, one that happens over and over again in things big and small, as we learn to yield our desires to His.

For me, this softening happened in small but noticeable increments. After I first became a believer and started attending a Bible-believing church, for those first few months I felt close to God all day on Sunday. Then the rest of the week happened, and God did not come close to registering on my radar. I didn't realize I should read my Bible or pray. Or at least make some sort of effort. Yet.

Eventually, slowly, that unmistakable closeness I sensed on Sunday lasted through all of Monday. Frankly, it felt bizarre. It seemed like God stood before me, smiling and waving, and I had to figure out what to do with that. It felt close to an imposition, yet my heart, with a mind all its own, responded. And as I learned to allow more of God into more of my life, a holy giving-way began to take place.

Before I knew it, I'd not only think of God on Monday, but also on Tuesday, Wednesday, and Thursday. I grew to anticipate the Lord's presence and, in a way that felt sort of like trying on a dress recommended by a friend that you never would have chosen but end up loving, I looked forward to our encounters. The last two days of the week were the last to fall, but fall they did, and I began to realize that God didn't want just part of me. He wanted all of me. He wants *all of us*. Every day.

It didn't take long for God to get down to business. He first pointed out an ongoing attitude issue, and I actually thought, *Wow, God showed me that wrong attitude, I repented, and I feel completely changed. Now I can go on with my life.* But just a couple of days later I felt the same holy tap on my shoulder and realized there was another issue God wanted to deal with. Then another. And yet another. I thought I must be in some sort of initial scrub stage, and God must be cleaning me up good. I figured within two or three weeks we'd be done with every potential issue, and I could proceed. (I am laughing as I type this. Oh, the absurd naiveté.)

After several months of the by now familiar holy shoulder-tapping, it dawned on me. This is not some sort of sacred initiation rite. This is how transformation happens. This is a holy, loving God working on my stubborn, ugly, issue-laden heart. God loves us so much He cannot bear for us to remain the way we've always been. And yes, He gives us a choice, but because His amazing love has already softened our hearts, we can't help but yield. We can't help but cooperate—even when it hurts.

This is not something we can conjure or force or manifest ourselves. As we learned in the Introduction, *the Holy Spirit will.* Everything God does is by His Spirit. His goal is to make us more and more like Him. And if our hearts are willing, we are changed—transformed from glory to glory by His Spirit. Remember, we are His image bearers (Genesis 1:26), and He wants us to reflect Him accurately and well.

This will probably sound dorky, but one of the first ways I noticed God changing me was through the radio. I stumbled onto a local Christian station and didn't hate it. In fact, I found the encouragement peculiarly welcome. I shocked myself, and it felt strange listening, yet I felt drawn in and eventually kept the dial tuned to that particular station.

> God loves us so much He cannot bear for us to remain the way we've always been.

His love for us is great and wonderful and intense. I was clueless that such love even existed. But as He pursued me and began softening my stony heart and enabled me to cooperate with Him, a breathtaking truth dawned. His love refreshes us, strengthens us, changes us, equips us, and utterly transforms us. His love never fails.

No wonder the enemy tries to erect barriers between us and God's love.

What Blocks His Love

If nothing separates us from God's love, why do we often feel so far from it?

For entirely too long, every time my husband and I had a blowout argument (which essentially happened every time we communicated—hence the long, somehow preferable stretches of painful silence), I always felt disconnected from God. Our dysfunction consistently took a painful emotional toll on me. As I look back, I realize that deep emotional wounds were in play, and the shame and distress I suffered acted as a massive crater of guilt and unworthiness in my mind. Overwhelming disappointment in my marriage and my own sinful responses and attitudes convinced me that God was certainly angry with me, not to mention fed up. How could He possibly love me when by my responses I'd let us both down? Over and over?

It's hard to sense God's love when you just screamed in retaliation at your husband, whose unkind words felt like a dagger going through your heart.

Hurt + guilt = mandatory separation from God (in my mind).

Though my heart genuinely desired to tiptoe close to Him, I couldn't fathom risking the approach. I stood condemned. Fear, coupled with all of my glaring shortcomings, glued my feet to a place far from Him.

Have you ever noticed that the enemy tends to attack our hearts in an already guilt-soaked area? We know the vile accusations are true, so we condemn ourselves by agreeing with the enemy and slink further from the One who possesses the power to not only forgive and cleanse us, but the authority to halt the enemy's tactics. The enemy's lambasting leads to feelings of rejection and isolation.

But that's not how our heavenly Father works at all. His conviction always arrives wrapped in gentleness and love. And though we will instantly recognize that His tender words of discipline are true, His Spirit draws us near so we can receive help and forgiveness for our failures. He makes us right with Himself!

> Who dares accuse us whom God has chosen for his own?
> No one—for God himself has given us right standing with
> himself (Romans 8:33).

In other words, even when we strongly sense those accurate accusations from the enemy (or our own conscience), if we ask for forgiveness, God Himself has already intervened, forgiven us, and made us 100 percent right with Himself. Satan instills fear that our sinfulness separates us from God's love. He paints an inaccurate picture in our hearts and minds that God is an angry God (or fill in your misguided and inaccurate version of God here), and that creates a fear of holy intimacy.

But that's not how love works at all. In fact, authentic love and fear cannot coexist; perfect love squelches fear.

> Such love has no fear, because perfect love expels all fear. If we are afraid, it is for fear of punishment, and this shows that we have not fully experienced his perfect love. We love each other because he loved us first (1 John 4:18-19).

I lacked the understanding and knowledge and experience of Christ's love. Because my earthly father had a serious rage issue, any infraction by my siblings or by me could trigger a volcanic reaction. Deep down part of me still subconsciously anticipated those same volatile reactions and projected them onto my perfect heavenly Father.

Though years later as an adult believer I forgave my dad, my past had created deep ruts in my very being. I was consistently tripped up by insecurity due to my own lack of experience with love, tenderness, and feeling valued. Clearly, these things interfered with my marriage relationship. On top of that, my shell-shocked heart remained ill equipped to respond to the idea of a loving God who had already given everything for a relationship with me.

God is the opposite of the earthly father I grew up with. He is slow to anger and abounding in love (see Psalm 103:8). My heart just didn't know that yet. That's why it's so important for us to take time and make time to know God for ourselves. We will learn that He is kind and loving and slow to anger as we study His Word and become familiar with His character.

It enables us to distinguish truth from error and to demolish every stronghold in our minds—including the ones that have been there for as long as we can remember.

> We use God's mighty weapons, not worldly weapons, to knock down the strongholds of human reasoning and to destroy false arguments. We destroy every proud obstacle

that keeps people from knowing God. We capture their rebellious thoughts and teach them to obey Christ (2 Corinthians 10:4-5).

As we practice learning to capture rogue thoughts, we are more able to accurately recognize His love at work. Even when we mess up. None of us gets it right 100 percent of the time. As James 3:2 puts it, "We all often stumble and fall and offend in many things" (AMPC). This verse points out what my heart already knows so very well: I frequently mess up. It's never my goal or intent, but it sure happens.

But though our hearts accuse us (and boy, mine sure does on *those* days…), God is greater than our hearts.

> We are of the Truth, and can reassure (quiet, conciliate, and pacify) our hearts in His presence whenever our hearts in [tormenting] self-accusation make us feel guilty and condemn us. [For we are in God's hands.] For He is above and greater than our consciences (our hearts), and He knows (perceives and understands) everything [nothing is hidden from Him] (1 John 3:19-20 AMPC).

What a blessed, glorious relief. Nothing is hidden from God. Not our efforts, our attempts, our failures. Not even our disappointment in ourselves. He is greater than all the repulsive junk that tends to accumulate in our hearts like so much smoke residue. And He knows that deep down we long to please Him, but our humanity often gets in the way.

When we turn to Him, in His vast loving-kindness He embraces us, then gently removes the *lame* sticky note from our foreheads and even plants a kiss there. Because He loves us. Because we are His. And though we mess up, He understands, and He forgives us when we ask. And I ask. A lot.

> If we [freely] admit that we have sinned and confess our sins, He is faithful and just (true to His own nature and promises) and will forgive our sins [dismiss our lawlessness] and [continuously] cleanse us from all unrighteousness

[everything not in conformity to His will in purpose, thought, and action] (1 John 1:9 AMPC).

We are imperfect, clinging to *His* perfection. Clinging to His unfailing love.

So even in the midst of those seasons when our insides feel like they're crumbling, when it feels like our mistakes are tallying up faster than votes on Election Day, when our hearts keep track of every single mess-up (why, oh why do we do that to ourselves?), we can run to His perfection, confident that He is far greater. He sits in the place of honor at God's right hand, pleading for us (Romans 8:34).

No Excuses

Sometimes our opinion of ourselves actually hinders us from accepting the unfathomable love Jesus offers. Our view of ourselves—and it may be an accurate view, when we know what a hot mess we really are—turns into an excuse. And we end up missing out.

This is how I lived for years. My head understood all God offered, but my heart condemned me. I hated how I sometimes responded to certain situations. I hated that anger kept me wound up tighter than a sailboat's ropes in a fierce storm. And the guilt over these (and other matters—lots of other inner matters) assured me I dare not even dream that I might be acceptable—let alone invited.

God gives us His love, but we have to actually accept it. And the primary excuse for me that was so deeply ingrained it existed on an almost subconscious level? *God couldn't possibly love me when I _____.*

I was missing out on so much of what the Lord offered me. So much of what, ironically, would have helped and healed me. Self-condemned and ashamed, excuses erupted out of me.

Jesus spoke of a man who prepared a sumptuous feast and sent out invitations. But every single person had an excuse why they couldn't attend (Luke 14:16-20). The excuses offered were more the busyness of life, but I firmly believe our hearts can drum up excuses equally—if not more—legitimate. *I'm too this. I'm not enough that.* Either way, excuses often prevent us from accepting all God offers us.

Yet Psalm 103 encourages us not to forget God's many benefits. When we know Him and love Him and live for Him, giving Him full access to our hearts, then His benefits, like His faithful presence, are there. Just waiting for us.

Back to the story of the man who sent out all the invitations. As the list of excuses piled up, he decided to extend his invitation beyond the original guest list. And this is where you and I come in.

> The servant returned and told his master what they had said. His master was furious and said, "Go quickly into the streets and alleys of the town and invite the poor, the crippled, the blind, and the lame." After the servant had done this, he reported, "There is still room for more." So his master said, "Go out into the country lanes and behind the hedges and urge anyone you find to come, so that the house will be full" (Luke 14:21-23).

This is God's heart for us. He knows good and well we're a hot mess, and He loves us anyway! Though our hearts are crippled, the eyes of our understanding are blind, and our souls are lame, He invites us. When shame pushes our hearts into hiding, He calls to us, inviting us in to an extravagant feast He has prepared just for us.

He longs to dine with us—to spend time with us and lavish us with His love. He calls us His children and gives us His unfailing love. The apostle John writes, "See how very much our Father loves us, for he calls us his children, and that is what we are!" (1 John 3:1).

When we refuse to make excuses and simply accept our King's invitation, we will be well-fed, satisfied, and nourished with the truth that He loves us. He will always love us. His banner over us is always, always love.

His Love Is Our Oasis

I discovered that I could run to the Lord when I felt misunderstood, wounded, or upset in any way. That happened a lot. He became the secret fortress I raced toward when things got ugly and my overwhelmed heart couldn't endure the pain. In the middle of our guilt, our doubts, our failures, His unfailing love is a lush, restorative oasis.

His love provides the comfort and security our hearts yearn for; it is a retreat we can escape into during our hardest moments. Just like when I was a girl visiting my grandparents' home, I found a beautiful, refreshing oasis existed in Christ. He is our safe place. As the psalmist says, "The LORD is my rock, my fortress, and my savior; my God is my rock, in whom I find protection. He is my shield, the power that saves me, and my place of safety" (Psalm 18:2).

He is the abode where our needs are met, and our wounds soothed, an inviting place where we are cherished and secure. Jesus invites us not just to visit this special place, but to dwell there. He can actually be our dwelling place, and He has been just that since even before King David wrote about it (Psalm 90:1).

A dwelling place is not just somewhere we occasionally visit. It can become our living space, our home. It's where our stuff is, where our hearts are at ease, and where we relax and are refreshed. In this place, our hearts and emotions are stabilized. But we don't automatically dwell with the Lord; we have to actually *go* to Him. We must be willing to regularly meet God, not just in the hard times, but in the good times too, until we are no longer just going there, but we abide there.

> If you live in Me [abide vitally united to Me] and My words remain in you and continue to live in your hearts, ask whatever you will, and it shall be done for you (John 15:7 AMPC).

Picture a beautiful tower attached to a breathtaking, massive main castle, yet completely separate, with its own separate door. And you are the only one who holds the key. The place is yours and yours alone. It's beautifully decorated to your personal taste with every comfort you could desire: a cozy chair, beautiful rug, a pair of those super-plush, fluffy socks, a lovely fireplace, and all the fixings for tea (or coffee). There's even a chocolate stash. It's a holy, inviting respite from the cares of the world. Best of all, Jesus meets you there. He holds you when you hurt. He rejoices with you when you're happy. He's faithful and steadfast, and His favorite thing on the planet is to spend time with you there, in your special, private dwelling place.

Jesus creates this sacred place for us to dwell in Him because He knows there will be times we desperately need it. It's the deep place in Him, where the deep places of our heart connect to the deep places of His. Because this is a refuge and fortress, the enemy cannot find us.

David knew this place well. Though King Saul sought his life, and David was forced to hide in caves for a lengthy period of time, his real hiding place was in the Lord. He remained there until the storms blew over. It's the same for us. God literally shelters us until our calamities are over.

> Be merciful and gracious to me, O God, be merciful and gracious to me, for my soul takes refuge and finds shelter and confidence in You; yes, in the shadow of Your wings will I take refuge and be confident until calamities and destructive storms are passed (Psalm 57:1 AMPC).

Back then, though I often *felt* separated from God, that wasn't an accurate reflection of the truth. We have to learn that though our emotions are powerful, they aren't always a correct indicator of the truth. And God never leaves us. We must understand that our situations— painful as they are—never separate us from God's love.

> For He [God] Himself has said, I will not in any way fail you nor give you up nor leave you without support. [I will] not, [I will] not, [I will] not in any degree leave you helpless nor forsake nor let [you] down (relax My hold on you)! [Assuredly not!] (Hebrews 13:5 AMPC).

Though He never leaves us, I had to learn to allow the circumstances to propel me *toward* the God who refused to leave me, instead of allowing them to pin my feet to the floor far from Him. I had to learn that Jesus always awaits me in that beautiful castle tower, arms outstretched.

I believe that God gave me my oasis summers and occasional weekends with my grandparents because He loved me. In His great kindness, He gave me respite. And even now, HE is our oasis. He is our shelter in the storm, our shade, our dwelling place.

I learned that in spite of the pain and the mess, He had in fact through His sacrifice made this hot mess more than a conqueror, and made it clear that nothing, nothing, nothing could separate me from His amazing love.

Do we believe that Jesus loves us so much that nothing can separate us from His love? When we're battling fear, discouragement, loneliness, and frustration, and when we feel so far away from Him our hearts echo, do we dare to believe His love has not budged a millimeter?

God doesn't love us because we're perfect. He loved us and sent His perfect Son to perfectly cover us—and cover every sin we would ever commit. Love covers! (1 Peter 4:8). Though sometimes our actions make us feel like unworthy paupers wearing filthy rags, in His great love the Lord covers us with holy, fresh, clean clothing.

> I will greatly rejoice in the Lord, my soul will exult in my God; for He has clothed me with the garments of salvation, He has covered me with the robe of righteousness, as a bridegroom decks himself with a garland, and as a bride adorns herself with her jewels (Isaiah 61:10 AMPC).

His Love Changes Everything

How different would we be if we knew—*absolutely knew*—that nothing could separate us from God's love? Can we say, along with Paul...

> I am convinced that nothing can ever separate us from God's love. Neither death nor life, neither angels nor demons, neither our fears for today nor our worries about tomorrow—not even the powers of hell can separate us from God's love. No power in the sky above or in the earth below—indeed, nothing in all creation will ever be able to separate us from the love of God that is revealed in Christ Jesus our Lord (Romans 8:38-39).

God's love and us? Undeniably, unequivocally, unquestionably inseparable.

How much more confident, stable, secure, and joyful would we be if we truly believed that? What if our roots grew deep down into God's love and kept us strong, and no circumstance could change that? What if we actually experienced His unfathomable, unfailing, unbelievable love for ourselves until it utterly transformed us, and we dripped with a holy residue that left its mark everywhere we ventured?

We each have a fundamental need to know—truly know, intimately, and for ourselves—that we are loved with an authentic, jealous, fiery, all-encompassing love. That we are loved by the One who declares, "Yes, I have loved you with an everlasting love" (Jeremiah 31:3 AMPC).

It's my fervent prayer that we truly understand and personally experience the full measure of Christ's love and experience it—for ourselves—in practical and deeply meaningful ways that lead to beautiful, God-honoring transformation into His image. When we are rooted deeply in God's love, experiencing it firsthand, it not only heals us and transforms us, it makes us more like Him.

> May you experience the love of Christ, though it is too great to understand fully. Then you will be made complete with all the fullness of life and power that comes from God (Ephesians 3:19).

What a breathtaking thought: We are made complete through His fullness of life. His power. His love. When we dare to believe and accept God's love for us, it rushes in and covers us, frees us, and transforms us. We become like Him—like love—because we will be filled with God Himself. God is love. And love never fails.

Every one of us should make it a goal to become intimately familiar with Christ's amazing love. A love that held nothing back. A love that saw us far ahead of time and deemed us worthy of an unimaginable price. It sounds flat crazy but I'm telling you, that holy goal will lead to His mighty, unfailing love pouring into every molecule of our being. And that is where authentic healing and transformation happen. Because in spite of our glaring imperfections, not one of them can separate us from His unfailing love.

Can anything ever separate us from Christ's love? [*Can being a hot mess?*] Does it mean he no longer loves us if we have trouble or calamity, or are persecuted, or hungry, or destitute, or in danger, or threatened with death?... No, despite all these things, overwhelming victory is ours through Christ, who loved us. And I am convinced that nothing can ever separate us from God's love. Neither death nor life, neither angels nor demons, neither our fears for today nor our worries about tomorrow—not even the powers of hell can separate us from God's love. No power in the sky above or in the earth below—indeed, nothing in all creation will ever be able to separate us from the love of God that is revealed in Christ Jesus our Lord (Romans 8:35-39, italics mine).

Are we convinced? Convinced that His love is greater than all the hurts and insecurities that threaten to cripple our hearts?

It astonishes me to know that amid all our guilt, our shame, and the deep emotional wounds that are major heart obstacles; amid all our junk, all our baggage, all our erroneous thinking; amid all our warped, inaccurate perceptions, Jesus's mighty love bursts in and brings what we desperately need: freedom. Freedom from the concrete barriers erected around our hearts. Freedom from the lie that we aren't good enough. Freedom from all of our guilt, our doubts, our massive failures.

This mighty love changes us. It obliterates our guilt, our doubts, and our failures. It is the massive, unshakable foundation upon which we stand, upon which our hearts are forever secure and brave and utterly, beautifully accepted and cherished.

His love changes everything.

Your Personal Proclamation:
SAY IT. KNOW IT. BELIEVE IT.

I accept and receive the awesome love of God. I will not make excuses. I will not come into agreement with the enemy's accusations. I believe God's love is at work in me, softening my heart and transforming me in many and various ways. His mighty love obliterates every barrier erected by my guilt, my doubts, and my failures. His unfailing love is at work in me and changing me.

I know that I am loved with an everlasting love that will never end. God's love makes me feel cherished, safe, and secure. His love is my comforting, refreshing oasis, and His banner, which waves over me every moment, is love. This mighty, unfailing love frees me from all my fears, makes me brave, and covers and frees me. Nothing in all creation can separate me from the love of God which is in Christ Jesus.

10

It's Not the CIA, but Special Assignments Abound

YOU ARE A WOMAN OF DESTINY

I tell you the truth, you can say to this mountain, "May you be lifted up and thrown into the sea," and it will happen. But you must really believe it will happen and have no doubt in your heart.

MARK 11:23

Knees trembling, I stepped into the big, bad, scary writers conference and took a shaky breath. Why on earth God would ask a high school dropout to write a book was beyond me. It made no sense to my mind, but my convinced heart didn't care. It just knew I was supposed to be there.

For years the Lord had spoken to me through a series of dreams (apparently, my brain is more accessible while I sleep). Over and over I had the similar dreams, and finally, through much prayer and thought, the significance and meaning of the dreams surfaced: God had entrusted me with the gift of communication. But due to the trauma of my early life, that gift had been not only buried, but utterly forgotten.

Buried Gifts

It's one of our adversary's stealthiest plans: to create a continual onslaught of heartache, pain, and trauma early on (or at any time,

177

really) so that we essentially live in crisis mode and never discover our gifts. Or we give up, relinquish, or even forget about the gifts He has given us.

My youthful love for writing was soon smothered by the ugliness of life. Hard as it is for me to believe now, as a young adult I lived my life in complete oblivion to my original dreams and without awareness of the gifts God had given me. Occasionally, I would read an article that posed questions about goals and dreams, but frankly, my heart and mind were completely out of touch with those long-forgotten desires. Once my gifts were buried, I truly forgot them.

Until Jesus gently nudged my heart. He never forgets the gifts He has bestowed to each of us, and His fervent desire is that we recognize them, nurture them, and use them for God's glory. And once God gives us gifts, He never takes them back.

> God's gifts and His call are irrevocable. [He never with-draws them when once they are given, and He does not change His mind about those to whom He gives His grace or to whom He sends His call.] (Romans 11:29 AMPC).

Even when our destinies lie submerged beneath years of ick, God doesn't change His mind about the gifts He has entrusted to us. He has the ability to softly stir our hearts; He coaxes our once-vibrant dreams out of dormancy, reawakening His purposes within us. He convinces us that our unique giftings, though once buried, are very much alive and waiting.

Specific Gifts, Specific Assignments

If I had to choose a favorite book of the Bible, it would most likely be Genesis. It's a fascinating look at the beginning of our earth and of time itself. I love to think about how crisp and new everything looked before skyscrapers and toxic chemicals and pollution existed. Imagine the night sky! With no electric lights shining on every street, it must have been a breathtaking sight. No wonder David speaks of the stars so often in the book of Psalms. Then I wonder about how pristine the air must have smelled, and how much more pleasant and appetizing the food tasted way back when everything was fresh and new (and organic!).

I find particularly intriguing the lists of firsts presented in Genesis. We discover the first herdsman who lived in a tent, Jabal. It may not sound all that impressive, but Jabal dreamed up and then designed and used the very first tent, enabling him to enjoy certain comforts of home while he followed his herds. (His wife no doubt thought him a genius!)

Then there's Tubal-cain, who was the first to work with metal. He forged tools of bronze and iron, probably creating the first knives and swords. Think about how much easier it was to butcher animals, chop wood, and even slice fruit after Tubal-cain's brilliant inventions.

We also meet Jubal, who holds the unique distinction of being the very first musician on the earth. Jubal (who was Jabal's brother and Tubal-cain's half brother), actually invented the harp and the flute (see Genesis 4:20-22). Let yourself think about the remarkable creative intricacies involved in dreaming up and then designing a musical instrument that had never before been seen or heard. Jubal not only designed and fashioned the first musical instruments, he then learned to play the instruments without instruction from another musician. How thrilling it must have been to hear those very first musical notes! I can almost see the wonder on the faces of Jubal's family hearing music for the first time.

What an amazing season of God pouring out His creative powers directly into His people. There is absolutely no denying that God supernaturally endowed each of these persons with unique, specific skills and abilities commensurate with the callings on their lives. They weren't taught by anyone who already knew the trade. They didn't intern somewhere or graduate cum laude from an Ivy League college. They simply operated in their natural gifts.

God provided good gifts to each of the men mentioned above. And He does the same for us. He uniquely gifted me—and you—with the exact qualities we would need to fulfill the precise callings for every season of our lives. Jabal, Tubal-cain, and Jubal all recognized and then used the gifts God poured into them. What marvelous examples of God's creative gifts put to good use.

God still gives talents and abilities. Some well-known examples include Mozart, who expertly composed music and performed before royalty starting at the tender age of five. Once he visited the Sistine Chapel, where he heard Allegri's *Miserere* performed, and later he wrote out the whole score from memory. Or consider Helen Keller. Struck deaf and blind through illness at the tender age of one, she went on to master Braille, touch-lip reading, typing, and finger spelling. Helen graduated cum laude from Radcliffe at the age of 24, spoke out on behalf of those living with disabilities, and later wrote her fascinating autobiography, *The Story of My Life*. Or scientist, inventor, and linguist Alexander Graham Bell, who held 18 patents and worked extensively with the deaf (including Helen Keller). He figured out how to send more than one telegram at a time, which ultimately led to the invention of the telephone.

We may not compose or invent or win science awards, but every one of us possesses particular talents and abilities, and we each have specific life assignments. We are endowed by our Creator with distinct gifts that will not only honor Him, but will give us a supreme sense of satisfaction when they're properly used.

There is a time and a season for everything, including the various assignments God has for us in the different seasons of our lives. Through prayer and the Holy Spirit's guidance, we are led toward and equipped for the specific tasks He has prepared for us. If God has given us curious minds, we must challenge ourselves and learn. If God has given us the gift of hospitality, we must invite others into our homes. If He has given us the ability to sing or run or teach or create or manage a business, we will be most satisfied when we use what He has provided.

Whatever our assignment, we will do well to remember that it's not people for whom we work, but God Himself. When we use our God-given abilities to work for Him and not for people, He is glorified. Paul reminds us to "work willingly at whatever you do, as though you were working for the Lord rather than for people" (Colossians 3:23).

How thrilling to ponder the fact that God wrote all our days before we drew our first breath. He created specific tasks and projects for us to accomplish while we're here on earth. And while freedom of choice always reigns, I want my life to as closely match what He laid out as possible. Psalm 139:16 reminds us, "You saw me before I was born. Every day of my life was recorded in your book. Every moment was laid out before a single day had passed."

Not "laid out" as in we're all robots blindly beeping through what we've been programmed to do, but we are presented with divine, destiny-filled opportunities, appointments, and moments laid out beautifully and precisely for the unique gifts and callings God created for us. The very ones He had in mind when He created me—and you.

> We are God's [own] handiwork (His workmanship), recreated in Christ Jesus, [born anew] that we may do those good works which God predestined (planned beforehand) for us [taking paths which He prepared ahead of time], that we should walk in them [living the good life which He prearranged and made ready for us to live] (Ephesians 2:10 AMPC).

Having said that, I do take incredible comfort in knowing that when our choices oppose His will (either before or after we know Him, because God is faithful like that), He nonetheless beautifully weaves all the frayed edges and creates a masterpiece.

I don't ever want to take my destiny lightly. Jesus paid a high price for my freedom, and I want to be a wise, faithful steward of all He has entrusted to me. My life is worth nothing if I don't finish the tasks God has designated for me. Like the apostle Paul, we must understand that our lives absolutely hold divine purpose. In Acts 20:24 he said, "My life is worth nothing to me unless I use it for finishing the work assigned me by the Lord Jesus—the work of telling others the Good News about the wonderful grace of God."

Paul's assignment was to tell others the Good News. It is an assignment we all share. Yet whether our specific assignments are raising godly children, being a light in the marketplace, running a corporation, or baking cookies for our neighbors, God has established and preordained our gifts and the tasks He desires us to do. We would be wise to prayerfully consider where God wants us and what He desires us to do in each season of our lives.

But Stepping into Our Destinies Isn't Always Easy

So there I was, tiptoeing wide-eyed through my first writers conference, armpits soggy from the stress of it all, trying hard not to throw up or faint. And it didn't take long for my formerly convinced heart to wilt. All through the crowded hallways strolled confident, experienced, educated writer people. Authors. Editors. Even publishers.

I was totally out of my league.

It didn't help that the enemy continually pointed out my obvious shortcomings, and my insecurities only amplified his malicious words and my own misgivings. Satan's goal is to stop us from living the life God intended for us and to prevent us from glorifying God by using our gifts and talents for His honor. He wants to steal or destroy our destiny. If we're not careful, we will come into agreement with him, and that's a dangerous place to be. When we, through our doubts, insecurities, and wounds step into agreement with the enemy, we allow the thief entrance; we essentially give him permission to have his way.

The adversary's purposes are clear: He comes to "steal and kill and destroy" (John 10:10). The enemy *always* comes. He may leave for a bit and wait for a more opportune time (see Luke 4:13), but we should never be surprised at his arrival. This is why the apostle Peter entreats us to remain vigilant: "Stay alert! Watch out for your great enemy, the devil. He prowls around like a roaring lion, looking for someone to devour" (1 Peter 5:8).

Unfortunately, sometimes the enemy stealthily slips in—when we're worn down, overly busy, distracted, or just plain discouraged. When we agree with the enemy, even when it is inadvertent and we are not aware, by default we then step out of agreement with the Lord. But when we remain alert, we can recognize his approach, run to the Lord, resist the enemy, and stand firm.

The first key to remaining alert is to remain close to the Lord. He guides us into all truth (John 16:13), He is our help (Psalm 121:2), He is a shield around us (Psalm 3:3), and we find protection in Him (Psalm 2:12).

The second key to remaining steadfastly alert is to ask God to give us wisdom. He always does. And this holy wisdom equips us to actively stand against the enemy. It enables us to live lives that please God, bear fruit, and truly know Him.

> We ask God to give you complete knowledge of his will and to give you spiritual wisdom and understanding. Then the way you live will always honor and please the Lord, and your lives will produce every kind of good fruit. All the while, you will grow as you learn to know God better and better (Colossians 1:9-10).

Isn't that what we long for? To possess spiritual wisdom and understanding so that our very lives always honor and please God?

In spite of my writers conference trepidations, I managed to meet some wonderful people, including a small group of women who were all newer writers, like me. Yet when I discovered that each of them held some sort of college degree, my heart sank even more (as if it needed help). One woman held a master's degree in Journalism. Another had a bachelor's degree in English Literature. On and on it went. All around me smart, capable, well-educated writer people schmoozed and made appointments with editors. The more I heard, the louder my glaring inadequacies shrieked. If lack of confidence caused death, I would have expired right then and there, between the authors' book displays and the publisher appointments sign-up table.

Nerves prevented me from eating properly, and by the end of the second day I was convinced I'd made a huge mistake. Clearly, I didn't belong there. Everyone—and I mean *everyone*—clearly had a huge advantage over me: a college education.

That night I drove out of the conference parking lot, commuting back toward the haven of my home—the safe place where I knew how to do everything expected of me: laundry, dinner, errands, mopping, and home schooling. As I drove those back roads toward our house, I attempted to prayerfully process what God seemed to be requiring of me. As I prayed, all of my doubts, fears, and exasperation gushed out. Hot tears made driving difficult, but my overwhelmed heart couldn't hold back the deep doubts demanding expression, which sounded something like this:

Okay, God, this can't be right. I am overwhelmed by my own lack of experience and education. It's just not fair that You're apparently asking me to do something that smart, educated people do. I have no clue how to write! I do not understand! How am I supposed to do something I haven't even been trained for?

How many times have we asked God why He is requiring us to do something for which we feel entirely inadequate? After all, we don't feel prepared and lack training, so how could it possibly work? We're ill equipped. We have no credentials. We. Are. Clueless. And we feel foolish.

Yet God uses the foolish things of the world to confound the wise. And He chooses things that are powerless to shame those who are powerful (1 Corinthians 1:27).

Though everything in me wished I had somehow managed to attend college, I discovered that human credentials don't impress God, and He does not need them. I began to understand that my future and my potential were not held hostage by my past, my lack of education and experience, or even my own lack of confidence. As Paul reminded us, "God is not impressed with the positions that men hold and He is not partial and recognizes no external distinctions" (Galatians 2:6 AMPC).

I began to understand that the Lord wasn't asking me to do everything in my own strength (because clearly, I had none). Eventually, it dawned on me that if He could do anything, He could certainly help me do the thing(s) I didn't think I could...even writing. Deep down I desperately longed to obey God. So I made the decision to continue moving forward, obeying to the best of my ability.

Do we think Mary wasn't scared when she heard God's plan for her to bear the Savior of the world? Do we think she didn't struggle with the certain and unsettling awareness that as her midsection blossomed, her reputation would likely be as good as ruined? And what about all the other details that no doubt pummeled her mind and heart? Would Joseph think her a lying adulteress? Or flat crazy?

He Allows Us to Say No

God always allows us freedom of choice, but every choice we make has a consequence—either good or bad. King Saul learned that the hard way. God anointed him king (see 1 Samuel 10), yet through Saul's stubborn choices to do things his own way, he eventually lost the throne. God then chose David as Saul's replacement. We cannot stubbornly cling to our own ways without consequences. We must be willing to obey God even when we don't completely understand. Even when it means stepping out in faith without a clue.

God is still looking for those like David, who was a man after His own heart.

> But God removed Saul and replaced him with David, a man about whom God said, "I have found David son of Jesse, a man after my own heart. He will do everything I want him to do" (Acts 13:22).

Are we willing to do everything God wants us to do? Even when it's hard, when it doesn't always make complete sense to us, or when we feel utterly inadequate?

Every step of obedience I have taken in following God's revealed tasks for me has been painfully cautious because it was initially so difficult for me to fathom that God wanted me to write. But as I stepped out in faith, He always confirmed my way.

Even though it was scary and hard, something deep within me recognized His call. And I didn't want to ignore or disregard God's ultimate plans and purposes. He whispered and pulled me forward by the power of His Spirit. Through His effusive grace, God enabled me to perceive the right way to go. He helped me obey what I sensed Him calling me to do.

It's my prayer for you as I type these words. That God will enable you to sense the right way to go and give you great grace, courage, and boldness to do it with excellence so that not a jot or tittle of your destiny goes unwritten.

Like Saul, we can choose to ignore God's promptings and miss out on all He has planned for us. Or we can surrender our idealized version of how our lives should unfold and trust Him in spite of how we feel. We can wholeheartedly cooperate and embrace and pursue Him and His plans and purposes for our lives. We can work hard, trust that God is able to use us, and become women after God's own heart.

Even if His specific assignment makes us feel like the incredible shrinking woman.

When We Feel Microscopic

Sometimes God calls us to do big things. Like step out of comfortable and into crazy. Into what we've never done before. He calls us to believe the impossible. Nurture and use once-buried gifts. And chase after God-sized dreams. Like running a marathon. Or learning to fly an airplane. Or raising godly children with a passion for the things of God. Or even graduating from college when you're much older than all the other students. But daring to pursue big things is scary. Very scary. Heart palpitation scary. Even when we're trying to be brave. And that's when we can start to feel small. Miniscule. Microscopic. And completely inadequate for the task ahead of us.

I'm convinced that feeling small and inadequate is no sin. In fact, it's simply us facing the reality of our own humanity, frailties, and inadequacies. Because in the grand scheme of things, we *are* small. And often our best efforts *are* feebly inadequate.

That is probably how Joshua felt. He had big shoes to fill. After the death of Moses, he was the Israelites' new leader, and in spite of his training and the fact that God placed him in that position, he faced a daunting task that he probably wasn't sure he could handle (see Numbers 27:18-23).

Clearly, God does things His own way, far differently than we might anticipate. In fact, the divine mystery of God's power working best in weakness is something I'm still endeavoring to understand, even though I've experienced it for myself. The fact that God chose a high school dropout with zero confidence, zero experience, and zero clue to write books is just a smidgen of proof that God shows off best when He uses the least.

It's difficult to fathom that a perfect, holy God doesn't always choose to work through wise, powerful people with sterling reputations. He often chooses the lowliest (Gideon), the youngest (King David), those with no confidence (Moses), or those of ill repute (Rahab).

You may have noticed that 2 Corinthians 12:9 does not say, "My power works best in weakness *when you're not scared.*"

Often when we step out to use our gifts, fear slithers up right next to us. It's why David wisely stated, "When I am afraid, I will put my trust in you" (Psalm 56:3). It's not that we won't feel afraid. It's that we must not allow fear to prevent us from working on and completing our God-given tasks.

Sometimes God's assignments are not easy. Not pleasant. Not fun. And Lord knows, I'm all about the fun moments in life. But we live in reality, so we face health issues (check), child issues (check), work issues (check), or marriage issues (check check). When those crushing moments of intense opposition (which often unleash a herd of self-doubt) step between us and our gifts and destinies, we can take comfort in knowing we're not the only ones.

It almost seems wrong to feel relieved and an odd sense of camaraderie knowing someone else is going through all sorts of opposition too. That we're not the only ones targeted. But it's not wrong. It's a holy kinship born of hardship that happens when we step out to obey God. And it's during times like these when we learn to lean on God and spur one another on to do likewise. The apostle Paul gives it to us straight:

> We think you ought to know, dear brothers and sisters, about the trouble we went through in the province of Asia. We were crushed and overwhelmed beyond our ability to endure, and we thought we would never live through it. In fact, we expected to die. But as a result, we stopped relying on ourselves and learned to rely only on God, who raises the dead (2 Corinthians 1:8-9).

Do you ever wonder when we will learn to truly rely on the Lord? It's no doubt the primary reason God allows us to experience such crushing opposition.

Our fears may hinder us, but they are no hindrance to the Lord, Who can accomplish His purposes in spite of our fears (look what He did through Moses, who was too afraid to speak to Pharaoh). That's why God encourages us—actually, He commands us—to be strong and courageous: "This is my command—be strong and courageous! Do not be afraid or discouraged. For the LORD your God is with you wherever you go" (Joshua 1:9).

Over and over, in fact three times in the first chapter of Joshua alone, God commands Joshua to be strong and courageous. When we feel ill equipped and unable to handle the assignment(s) before us, God encourages us. He reminds us that through Christ we are, in fact, ready and able for anything.

> I have strength for all things in Christ Who empowers me [I am ready for anything and equal to anything through Him Who infuses inner strength into me; I am self-sufficient in Christ's sufficiency] (Philippians 4:13 AMPC).

The fact that God infuses His strength into us flat-out amazes me. His power is the bridge between the task(s) He has called us to accomplish and the reality of our human inabilities. He enables us to do what we could never do apart from Him.

But as I discovered when God whispered His baffling plans to my heart, it's hard to embrace the promise when we're busy looking at the facts.

When Facts Roadblock Us

Facts are tricky little things. Massive boulders of doubt that totally block the road before us. And I tend to trip over them or become flummoxed while attempting to figure out how to figure out my next step. Maybe your facts are similar to mine. Maybe you lack an education. Maybe your finances are iffy, or you lack some other critical component that (in the natural) you believe is necessary. Maybe you have no idea how the grand scheme of God's plans will unfold for you because (in the natural) there's just no way. Like me, maybe you have lots of blanks that have not yet been filled in.

And blanks are intimidating!

Yet whatever we consider our glaring shortcomings, those pesky facts are no match for God. They are certainly no hindrance. He is the One who parted the Red Sea. He is the One who used a virgin to give birth to His Son. He is the One who resurrects the dead. God isn't asking us to step out into our destinies and use the gifts He has entrusted to us when every *i* is dotted and every *t* crossed, and we're 100 percent confident. He is inviting us to step out in faith and trust Him to move supernaturally. Not because we're all that, but because He is.

Eventually, we must choose to come into agreement with what God makes clear to us or risk missing our destinies. We must surrender our overwhelming sense of inadequacy and believe God knows what He is doing. It's what He requires of us all—to accept His gifts and dare to believe that He could use someone like us. Jesus told us, "You didn't choose me. I chose you. I appointed you to go and produce lasting fruit, so that the Father will give you whatever you ask for, using my name" (John 15:16).

Lasting fruit is the work we do for the Lord in faith, with pure hearts and clean motives and through His supernatural help. It holds eternal value. It's our humble, obedient, grace-dependent response to His holy direction. It's how, when we breathe our last breath, we will be able to face Him and hear, "Well done, my good and faithful servant" (Matthew 25:23).

When we partner with Jesus and create lasting fruit we will (eventually) receive a reward.

> Anyone who builds on that foundation may use a variety of materials—gold, silver, jewels, wood, hay, or straw. But on the judgment day, fire will reveal what kind of work each builder has done. The fire will show if a person's work has any value. If the work survives, that builder will receive a reward. But if the work is burned up, the builder will

suffer great loss. The builder will be saved, but like someone barely escaping through a wall of flames (1 Corinthians 3:12-15).

Our Holy Potential

Remember Gideon? In the book of Judges, chapter six, we witness another angelic visit. Remarkably, the angel first announced who
Gideon was in God's sight, much to his surprise. In spite of the fact that
Gideon was hiding down inside a winepress to sift wheat—this out of
necessity, as the Midianites had destroyed their crops, and precious little food was available. Sifting wheat in a winepress may have been the
prudent thing to do, but it certainly wasn't the bravest. Yet God saw
Gideon's potential and spoke to it.

> And the Angel of the Lord appeared to him and said to him,
> The Lord is with you, you mighty man of [fearless] courage
> (Judges 6:12 AMPC).

The angel then gave Gideon his marching orders. Scary marching
orders. And Gideon could hardly believe his ears. Gideon's response?
"But…how can I?" (verse 15).

Gideon's question was the very same question I asked back on that
scary first day of the writers conference. And it's the same question Mary
asked when the archangel Gabriel announced God's stunning plan.

Isn't that the very question that pounds against our hearts when we
sense God speaking scary words of promise? Words that require effort
and cooperation and faith on our part, especially when we don't understand and when every cell in our bodies trembles with fear?

"How can I _____ when _____?"

Yet God saw something in Gideon. He saw his potential. And I'm
convinced He sees the potential in us too. If only we will rise to the
occasion.

We may not defeat the Midianites, but God still desires to accomplish specific, awesome things both in us and through us. Things for
which He has uniquely equipped us. Things that may not always

appear grand or flashy, yet if He is the Author and Establisher of those things, we can be assured they hold eternal value.

Everything God accomplishes in and through us matters. It all holds value and divine purpose. Even the nonglamorous things. The day-to-day things. The things we do that nobody ever sees. But God sees. And when we do each thing unto Him, He is not only honored, but greatly pleased.

God uses who He wants…He doesn't look for the talented so much as the willing. In both Gideon and Mary, He saw willing hearts. Not perfect hearts, but humble and willing hearts. And with those two qualities, God can do anything. Those two ingredients allow God to fill in every blank.

Doing Our Part

Through those dreams I spoke of at the beginning of the chapter, God faithfully whispered, and when I finally realized and recognized that He had given me the gift of communication, my stunned brain could scarcely comprehend it. And yet everything deep within me knew and (eventually) accepted this surprising truth.

As I pondered and prayed, I sensed the Lord asking me to nurture the writing gift and make it grow. To do my part and be faithful with the gift He had entrusted to me. God invites us not only to believe Him, but to do our part—to actively participate in fulfilling our destinies.

Sometimes our part will involve formal education, though the Lord is certainly able to equip us apart from that (remember Jubal and Tubal-cain and Jabal!). Sometimes God might lead us to attend conferences or join clubs or get involved in local community groups. He might bring a mentor into our lives for a season or teach us through life events, books, DVDs, or small groups. However God chooses to lead and train us, our job is to hear Him and obey Him.

The most vital aspect of nurturing the gifts God has entrusted to us is to cultivate our ability to accurately hear what His Spirit is saying specifically. Mark 4:9 says, "Anyone with ears to hear should listen and understand."

Whether God chooses to speaks to us through His Word, through dreams, circumstances, or those around us, or any of a hundred ways—however God chooses to speak—we must always actively cultivate ears that hear Him. This means that daily we purpose to align our hearts with His. Daily we ask Him to orchestrate every detail and help us to follow and obey Him. We daily and by His grace walk in the Spirit.

When we are controlled and guided by His Spirit, we won't get involved in things that don't concern us. We won't waste our time.

In other words, we won't indulge our bossy flesh.

Walking in the Spirit—daily hearing Him, yielding to Him, and remaining close to Him—enables us to be about our Father's business. It's how Jesus lived, how He accomplished everything that God required of Him.

God chose us, equipped us with specific gifts, and desires for us to produce fruit. Eternal fruit. Jesus has literally appointed us to produce lasting fruit using the gifts God has entrusted to us. He is interested in results that remain—results that matter in light of eternity. In addition, we are expected to use well what we are given, or it will be taken from us.

> To those who use well what they are given, even more will be given, and they will have an abundance. But from those who do nothing, even what little they have will be taken away (Matthew 25:29).

I want to be a faithful steward of what God has entrusted to me. I want to wisely use what I have been given, and I want to hear, "Well done, my good and faithful servant" (Matthew 25:23).

How about as we ponder and pray, we ask God to enable us to recognize and accept the gifts He has given us? How about if we choose to accept the gifts—no matter how surprising—and commit to doing our part?

What if, instead of agreeing with the enemy that there's just no way, we link arms with Jesus, Who *is* the Way? What if we determine to believe God is not only able to reveal our destinies, but to equip us in whatever way He sees fit and in His perfect timing? What if we step forward trusting Him instead of doubting ourselves?

Let's lay our humble and willing hearts before Him—those two beautiful ingredients with which Almighty God can supersede all we could ever dare to hope, ask, or imagine. Let's acknowledge that we are women in possession of divinely bestowed gifts and talents, with specific assignments. And let's dare to believe that we are, in fact, determined women of destiny.

Your Personal Proclamation:
SAY IT. KNOW IT. BELIEVE IT.

I have a God-given destiny, I possess divinely bestowed gifts and talents, and I intend to pursue and accomplish every God-given assignment with a humble and willing heart. I believe my destiny is in God's hands, but that I have an active role in it. I will not agree with the enemy and allow him access into my life but will daily walk with and remain near Almighty God.

I will not yield to feelings of inadequacy, stop at road-blocks, or allow myself to feel microscopic. I will do my part by daily being led, trained, and prepared by the Holy Spirit. God has entrusted me with specific, unique gifts, and I *will* use them for His glory. My life holds divine purpose, and I will, by God's effusive grace, accomplish all that He has for me on this earth.

11

It Surpasses Our Dreams in a Spectacular Sort of Way

I WILL BLESS YOU

❦

And Abram believed the LORD, and the LORD
counted him as righteous because of his faith.

GENESIS 15:6

If there's one thing I especially treasure, it is God's ability to speak to me when I most need it (even if I don't quite realize I need it), in the most unlikely places and times. In a restaurant, in a crowd of people, in the middle of an argument (thank God), He speaks. When my heart hurts so badly I can barely string together two coherent thoughts, He speaks.

I find it incredulous that when I'm irritated, when my attitude is embarrassingly wrong, when my heart is in turmoil, He speaks. But oh, I'm grateful. Hard to believe He speaks at such times? Consider that God spoke to Jonah even while he fumed (Jonah 4); He spoke to Job in the midst of all his awful turmoil (Job 38–41); and he spoke to Paul when his heart was right but his actions were dead wrong (Acts 9:3-6).

But on a Monday morning after a particularly unpleasant weekend, as I started my chores and stripped the creamy-white cover from my ancient bedroom prayer chair and tossed it into the wash, I hardly expected to hear from God. It was just a usual morning cleaning house—with a heavy heart.

Housework isn't my favorite thing, but housework with a heavy heart is far worse. It's hard to push a vacuum cleaner when you're carrying what feels like a 75-pound sack of wet sand across your back. That's where I was that morning. Struggling with old hurts that got tangled up with fresh wounds from a rough weekend marriage-wise, and cry-praying from room to room.

Cry prayers are depth-of-our-soul prayers—the ones that don't stand on ceremony or prayer etiquette 101. They're raw and gritty and authentic and are truly the deepest part of our hearts crying out to the deepest part of God's.

> O my God, my life is cast down upon me [and I find the burden more than I can bear]…[Roaring] deep calls to [roaring] deep at the thunder of Your waterspouts; all Your breakers and Your rolling waves have gone over me (Psalm 42:6-7 AMPC).

It's our hearts roaring out to His, crying out for relief when our souls are discouraged. Cry prayers even happen while we're doing chores, which you may consider strange. But if *in Him we live and move and have our being* (Acts 17:28), and we are to *pray at all times and on every occasion* (Ephesians 6:18), it all makes perfect, divine sense. And somehow I think these kinds of prayers touch God the most: honest prayers that open the sacred door of vulnerability, hold nothing back and, like a crazy person jumping off the seventeenth deck of an ocean liner, just dive in deep.

After tossing the chair cover into the washing machine, I wiped tears from my chin onto my sleeves and decided to scoot the chair aside and vacuum what turned out to be a small garden plot beneath it. That's when I noticed it. Buried beneath about a good inch of fluffy (but not in the good way) dirt, pet fur, and dust rested a forgotten 3x5 card. I knelt down and pinched the index card with the very tips of my fingers, lifting it out of the mess. I shook off most of the filth, blew off some more dust, and read it.

Fear not [Julie], I am your Shield, your abundant compensation, and your reward shall be exceedingly great (Genesis 15:1 AMPC).

And suddenly, I was knee-deep in grace.

In an unexpected place, with a heavy heart, and in enough layers of dirt a seed could have sprouted, God's word of promise appeared. And in that surprising moment, everything shifted.

That a beautiful, completely forgotten Scripture verse rose out of the dirt to speak to me touched me to tears. "When they walk through the Valley of Weeping, it will become a place of refreshing springs. The autumn rains will clothe it with blessings" (Psalm 84:6).

God spoke beautiful words in an ugly place, and in so doing spoke volumes to my aching, weary heart. It demonstrated so clearly that Almighty God was well acquainted with my hardship. That He noticed and understood. That as I walked through the Valley of Weeping, He saw and He sent the refreshing blessing of His Word. Suddenly, the 75-pound bag of wet sand was lifted off my shoulders, and I felt validated and understood and not at all alone. He lifted me, and the despair that vise-gripped my heart that day shook loose.

As easily as I lifted that 3x5 card, He lifts us. Over and over again, He places His hands on our weary selves. And though we grow exhausted, He never does. He never stops rescuing us. He lifts us and shakes off all the accumulated stuff and breathes on us, and suddenly we can breathe easier. We can see. He sends blessings of good things (Psalm 21:3). And our souls are reassured and at ease. His words lift us. They enable us to rise up out of our mood, our circumstances, our wrong attitude, the places of deep hurt. This spectacular fact overwhelms my heart until gratitude literally seeps out of every pore.

Yet rising above our circumstances is always a choice.

And choices can be harder than frozen concrete, especially when we've been down for a while. Sometimes we get comfortable in the bad place. We lose hope, grow complacent, and don't see the use in trying. Jesus noticed a man who fit that description, and He had a question for him. When we allow ourselves to wallow far too long, I think He poses this question to us:

> There was a certain man there who had suffered with a deep-seated and lingering disorder for thirty-eight years. When Jesus noticed him lying there [helpless], knowing that he had already been a long time in that condition, He said to him, *Do you want to become well?* [Are you really in earnest about getting well?] (John 5:5-6 AMPC, italics mine).

When the dirt scatters and the promise appears, do we truly want it? Are we willing to reach in and grab hold of it? Are we willing to embrace God's words of blessing, allowing His truth to shake off the dirt, realign our hearts, and completely change our perspective?

If you've ever dealt with an unwilling two-year-old, you know the mighty force of sheer toddler stubbornness. One tenacious, strong-willed child who doesn't *want* to pick up toys can suddenly grow limp legs, and then all bets are off. I don't want to be that stubborn toddler. I don't ever want to fold my arms in defiance and willingly remain in the mess I've made. I don't want a stubborn heart that demands its own way. I want a soft, willing heart that yields fully to God, along with eyes to see and recognize the blessings He has provided for me.

Are we willing to do our part without excuse, without casting blame, without growing limp legs? Are we willing to rise above the circumstances that have held us down for entirely too long?

> Arise [from the depression and prostration in which circumstances have kept you—rise to a new life]! Shine (be radiant with the glory of the Lord), for your light has come, and the glory of the Lord has risen upon you! (Isaiah 60:1 AMPC).

Yes, when light appears, dirt is visible to a greater degree. But there's a purpose in it—so that we can see the mess—see the depth of the dirt around and even within us. It motivates us to action. His beautiful light creates a desire to rise. Sort of like plopping down into a lawn chair at a summer barbecue only to realize it's covered in someone's spilled drink. We realize *we can't just sit in a mess*, and so we jump right back up, then grab some paper towels and get to work. We arise.

His Blessings, Our Promise

The verse I discovered that day on the 3x5 card as I knelt in the dirt on my bedroom floor took my breath away. God cared enough to not only meet me in my unlikely indoor garden plot, but His words of promise buoyed my heart. *That* is the power of God's Word. His very words bless us. Let's dive into it together.

> Fear not...I am your Shield, your abundant compensation, and your reward shall be exceedingly great (Genesis 15:1 AMPC).

He shields us. He covers and protects us, watching over us with mighty power and tender, loving care.

> The Lord is my Rock, my Fortress, and my Deliverer; my God, my keen and firm Strength in Whom I will trust and take refuge, my Shield, and the Horn of my salvation, my High Tower (Psalm 18:2 AMPC).

When life's dirt gets dumped on us, we have a place to run. He is our heart's fortress, the rock which stabilizes our sometimes feeble knees, the tower to which we can escape—high above life's most painful moments.

He compensates us. He Himself is our compensation—He blesses and compensates us for our trouble, our loss, our disappointment, and our grief with His beautiful presence. When we've been held in a difficult place—imprisoned by doubt, discouragement, insecurity, fear, or whatever it may be—His refreshing presence soothes us and gives our hearts the divine rest they desperately need.

And He rewards us. He notices our efforts, our hard work, and our diligence, and He actually rewards us. And His rewards are abundant: peace, joy, grace, contentment, soul satisfaction, and a deep inner sense of well-being that no circumstance can shake, just to name a few.

In an unlikely place, God spoke to my heart, encouraging me not to give up. Reminding me He would compensate me for all the pain. Telling me I could expect a reward—a great reward. He speaks to us in unlikely places the words our hearts desperately yearn to hear.

Isn't that what we crave? To know that all we're going through, all we're enduring as we strive to obey Him, honor Him, and do the right thing even when it costs us—especially when it costs us—is somehow going to make an eternal difference, and that God notices, that He sees, and, wonder of wonders, He rewards us?

We can know that God will somehow speak through the ick. That whatever ugly mess we're knee-deep in, His grace abounds and runs toward us and captures our hearts anyway. And "God will generously provide all you need. Then you will *always* have everything you need and plenty left over to share with others" (2 Corinthians 9:8, italics mine).

I guess what most touches my heart is that God speaks and blesses us with beautiful words at surprising times and in surprising places. Ugly places. He speaks and in that moment transforms an ordinary day or a hard season into one of promise and blessing. He speaks and transforms an ordinary *life* into a life of hope and promise and blessing.

We Must RSVP

If we want change, if we want His blessing, then we must first be eager to get up from where we have (knowingly or unknowingly) allowed our issues or circumstances to pin us. Fortunately for us, as His lights shines, it enables us to see where we have unwittingly cooperated with the enemy or allowed ourselves to be complacent or to wallow. Thank God for His light and truth flooding our hearts—sort of like a holy spotlight.

Then, when Jesus asks us, "Do you really want this?" we can truthfully answer in the affirmative because our hearts are ready. As we agree with and surrender to His Holy Spirit, we will begin to walk in everincreasing increments of freedom. His beautiful light covers us with stunning radiance that belies our circumstances. He lifts our hearts, our countenances, and the very depths of our souls. And authentic transformation begins.

He meets us right where we are, getting right down there in the dirt with us, but never, ever leaving us there.

Just because He blesses us doesn't mean it's easy. Change is arduous. Effort and hard work are involved. Yet, God never forces us—He invites us. He invites us to participate in the fresh, new things He envisions for our lives. We always have the "No" option. We can choose to remain in the dirt, in the old place, in the tired places. Or we can run with passion and joy to all that God is leading us toward—heading to the place He will show us.

That means He doesn't always provide detailed blueprints or even a map (and oh, how my inner organizer freak wishes He would!). It means sometimes the waters won't part until we take the first step. It's walking by faith, yet we *know* Him—we know He is faithful and utterly trustworthy (1 Thessalonians 5:24). We *know* nothing is impossible for Him (Matthew 19:26). We *know* He makes us as sure-footed as a deer, enabling us to stand on mountain heights (Psalm 18:33).

And knowing Him makes all the difference. It takes the fear out of going toward the unknown places. Even when we don't know the precise place we're headed, when we are led by His Spirit, we will always end up in the right place. And when we remain near Him, we are covered and protected and, most of all, we're stable. As the psalmist assures us: "He who dwells in the secret place of the Most High shall remain stable and fixed under the shadow of the Almighty [Whose power no foe can withstand] (Psalm 91:1 AMPC).

Even stable enough to walk on the water. Safe in the daring place among life's massive waves. Safe in the place no foe can withstand.

Leaving Ugly Behind

Abraham traveled toward an unknown destination. I think that describes us all. Not one of us knows what the future holds or where we will end up. But God knows.

> The LORD had said to Abram, "Leave your native country, your relatives, and your father's family, and go to the land that I will show you. I will make you into a great nation. I will bless you and make you famous, and you will be a blessing to others" (Genesis 12:1-2).

I believe there comes a time in each of our lives when God requires some form of change: behavior, attitude, thought, or heart change. He asks us to leave the old and go toward the new, which sounds exciting, but usually turns out to be a scary faith walk. Part of the reason it is scary is because walking in faith—not knowing where we're going—means we won't have GPS directions, and often it feels like we don't have a clue.

What we do have is Jesus, and the blessing and joy of His presence. He leads us by His Spirit, and as long as we remain near and keep our eyes focused on Him, we will eventually arrive at our divine destination.

Just like the Lord spoke to Abraham, His invitation to us is the same: *Leave your comfort zone. Leave your doubts behind. Leave your past in your past. Leave your former way of thinking. Leave the place where the enemy has held you for far too long.*

And leaving our familiar, comfortable places? It's exciting, yet scary. It's intimidating. And it feels flat crazy. Even when we *want* to leave, it's overwhelming to consider. Especially because, by God's design, we won't know exactly where we're headed. That part always makes my brain tilt.

It's a new place of utterly insane dependence on the Lord. A new era in our lives where we know He is the *only* way we will make it.

God desires for us to leave the familiar place of comfort, whether we're comfortable as cranky women, heartbroken women, hopeless women, or fearful women. I know…it's unimaginable one can become accustomed to and get comfortable in such ugly places, but it happens to all of us. Comfort turns into stuck. And like the man at the pool, years go by. He was there 38 years, waiting for someone to help him.

Jesus is our Someone.

But our rescue doesn't always look like we think. The invalid man lying at the pool of Bethesda never even reached his goal of getting in first after the angel stirred the waters. He simply did what Jesus told him, which *Tilt!* didn't involve stepping into the pool at all. But the man heard and he obeyed. It required action and effort on his part, and it's the same for us.

Years of trauma and neglect had taken a severe toll on my heart, and long after the worst of it was over, the worst of it was still in me.

My husband and I were in marriage counseling round seven. (We're nothing if not tenacious.) One evening, during a heated conversation in our living room, we hit a serious impasse, and my husband flatly announced that he didn't see any difference in my behavior as a believer. Indignant, I almost blew him off. But the Holy Spirit convinced me that there was a measure of truth in Keith's words. And oh, those words were hard to hear. Yet in a painful lesson, God gently revealed to me that my reactions and responses didn't always line up with what I claimed to believe. Youch.

Are we willing to hear what the Spirit of the Lord is saying to us? Do we really want to be well?

Over the next few days as I prayed, I realized that deep wounds had created a pool of ugly resentment and bitterness in my heart. The dichotomy of who I thought I was and how I sometimes acted hit me square in the face. No denying I was a hot mess. Clearly, repentance and forgiveness were in order, but I needed to choose them. And that's when I realized I needed to leave that place of my ugly. The place of my same old reactions. The place I felt entitled to.

One of the keys to obtaining God's blessing is obedience, and sometimes that involves the willingness to face facts we'd rather not and let go of our old ways so we can embrace the new. That's hard. We cling to the familiar because even when the familiar is less than God's best for us, the new is uncertain. There are no guarantees. And the transition between the two is nothing short of arduous.

The ultimate thing God requires us to leave behind is unforgiveness, which spellcheck insists isn't a word, but God (and my own heart) assures me exists. Part of cooperating with God involves truly forgiving. And I had no idea how deeply the releasing of those old wounds would hurt.

Letting go of our right to be right, letting go of resentments, letting go of the big walls we've held up for so long in an effort to protect ourselves? Excruciating. But we must relinquish our old mindsets, the former way of doing things. It's what God did in Abraham's life, and it's what He wants to do in ours.

What if, instead of allowing ourselves to maintain the status quo spiritually and emotionally and in all the stagnant areas, we recognized rogue attitudes in our hearts, or noticed when our minds took the less noble thought road? What if we asked God to help us recognize when it's high time to leave behind the old things so we're able to embrace the blessing of the new?

> Behold, I am doing a new thing! Now it springs forth; do you not perceive and know it and will you not give heed to it? I will even make a way in the wilderness and rivers in the desert (Isaiah 43:19 AMPC).

And Then We Go

God is inviting us out into the deep places no rational person would likely choose. The places where we are thrust into utter dependence on Him, and if He doesn't show up in a spectacular way, it's all over.

As I prayed about whether or not God was calling me to write this book, and whether or not I felt I was up to the task, I had a dream. I'd like to share it with you:

A Realtor friend and I sat on matching swings fastened to the bottom of a helicopter to get a great view of the area. (Strange, I know. It's a dream. Go with it.)

Hands gripping the swings' ropes, we were looking down at different homes when the helicopter veered toward the beach. Though I wasn't searching for a beach house, the bird's-eye view was spectacular, the beach cottages charming. Then we continued on and flew over the golden beach packed with families and dotted with colorful umbrellas and beach towels. To my surprise, we continued flying out past the beach, over the ocean.

Deeper and deeper out over the ocean we flew, and I began to grow uneasy. About three miles offshore, I gasped. There in the ocean depths stood massive condominiums, businesses, even single-family homes. The buildings swayed slightly in the water as massive waves splashed up against them, yet I knew the buildings were secure and safe. Still, I looked over at my friend and said, "I'm not so sure about this. I like terra firma. And I prefer a yard." Clearly, the people who lived in those buildings had no yard at all. Just deep, deep water surrounding their buildings, and enormous waves beating against the walls of their buildings.

I awoke from this unusual dream with the God-given realization that the Lord was calling me out of my comfort zone and into the deep—to places I would never go on my own—far from the safety that the shore represented. And He was inviting me to not merely fly over or visit the deep places but to *live there.* To abide with Him in the places I could never manage apart from Him.

I believe God is calling His women out into the deep—the scary places we might never go without His prompting. He is inviting us to leave our places of comfort, to leave the hurts and wounds and sins that cling to us like wet clothing, to let go of every encumbrance and be released from every obstacle so we can soar freely with Him.

We can *live* out in the deep. It's a place of unimaginable risk and unimaginable blessing that requires unimaginable faith. But it's in this place we can embrace the blessings that come with the territory and *live* in the place of radical faith and radical blessing.

The beautiful part is we do not go alone. God offers us the faithful assurance of His mighty presence.

> [God] Himself has said, I will not in any way fail you nor give you up nor leave you without support. [I will] not, [I will] not, [I will] not in any degree leave you helpless nor forsake nor let [you] down (relax My hold on you)! [Assuredly not!] (Hebrews 13:5 AMPC).

This holy promise is a spectacular truth my mind can scarcely comprehend. Family and friends fail us. People leave us and let us down. Promises are broken. But God always, always stays. He always supports us. He never leaves us helpless or forsakes us or lets us down. He never relaxes His hold on us.

While at the beach, I watched a father standing waist-deep in the surf, calling for his young daughter to join him. The sweet little girl cautiously observed the waves and then her daddy. Though she appeared uncertain, her father's outstretched arms, broad smile, and ultimately, I am convinced, knowing and trusting her daddy finally convinced her it was safe to jump into the waves. And jump she did.

God invites us to take the plunge to a place we might not ordinarily go—a place where waves of uncertainty attempt to undermine our confidence. Yet simple trust enables us to venture out, take the plunge, and jump into the waves of His blessings and promises. His strength and power and grace are our assurance. When we step out in obedience, He sustains and supports us.

How can we become new creatures if we're not willing to let go of the things God is clearly showing us to leave, and go to the new place waiting ahead? If the fresh and new has come, shouldn't we make way for it? Shouldn't we not only expect but accommodate the new things Christ desires?

> If any person is [ingrafted] in Christ (the Messiah) he is a new creation (a new creature altogether); the old [previous moral and spiritual condition] has passed away. Behold, the fresh and new has come! (2 Corinthians 5:17 AMPC).

Are we willing to turn toward Him with our new, clean hands and pure hearts, step away from the safe and known toward the new destination that initially feels scary or flat crazy? Because we can't get to the new place awaiting us until we relinquish the old place. We must leave the old behind, often without the assurance of knowing precisely where we're headed. And when we do, we will receive the Lord's blessing, so it's less fear factor and more holy adventure. As Psalm 24:5 says, "They will receive the Lord's blessing and have a right relationship with God their savior."

Now Look Up

God wants to transform our vision, increase our expectations, and increase our faith. He asks us to step outside the restrictive limitations we've tolerated and accept the unlimited potential He offers. He did it for Abraham, and He does the same for us:

> He brought him outside [his tent into the starlight] and said, Look now toward the heavens and count the stars— if you are able to number them. Then He said to him, So shall your descendants be. And he [Abram] believed in

(trusted in, relied on, remained steadfast to) the Lord, and
He counted it to him as righteousness (right standing with
God) (Genesis 15:5-6 AMPC).

Picture the scene. Abraham lifts his tent flap and, with an air of
expectancy, steps out into the crisp night. A warm wind blows as his
eyes adjust to the inky darkness. Slowly, he tilts back his head, his eyes
move up toward the stunning night sky, and his breath catches. Suddenly, Abraham begins to understand. Billions of stars sparkle, wholly
filling his field of vision. Mouth agape, both his mind and his heart
begin to respond as he attempts to comprehend the vast, limitless possibilities God is offering him.

Abraham probably wrestled initially, as we all do, to believe. It was
a stunning promise. But ultimately, Abraham realized that God was
capable of doing exactly what He said. What about the promises we
sense God has spoken to our hearts?

It's amazing to me that Abraham never wavered. How? How was
Abraham able to maintain such a deep and abiding faith in the One
who had made such stunning promises? It's simple, actually. Abraham
knew God. He trusted Him. He was utterly convinced that God could
do whatever He said.

Are we as certain?

> Abraham never wavered in believing God's promise. In fact,
> his faith grew stronger, and in this he brought glory to God.
> He was fully convinced that God is able to do whatever he
> promises (Romans 4:20-21).

When we refuse to waver and continue to trust God, our faith actually increases. And isn't that what we yearn for? We long to be women
who dare to believe. In spite of adverse circumstances. In spite of the
enemy's attempts to bring doubt and discouragement. Our focus, our
goal, our intent is to be women who dare to believe God can and will
bless us.

The Lord brought Abraham outside his tent so that he could see. I
believe the Lord does the same with us. He brings us out of our limited

perspectives and out of the old. The old places we've dwelt in for too long—that have held us back, whether in our minds or our emotions or whatever. God invites us to look up, away from the circumstances that have held our attention for far too long, away from the discouragement and the disappointment and toward the limitless possibilities He offers. He takes our hand, parts the tent curtain, and leads us out.

Out of what, exactly? Out of our limited viewpoints, our small way of thinking, our erroneous thinking, the hurts from our past, the bondage the enemy hopes we will never escape, the heartache, the disappointments which have confined us for so long. He brings our hearts and minds outside of the situations and circumstances around which we have pitched our tents of woe. He takes us outside of ourselves, outside of our natural limitations, outside of our comfort zones.

And in bringing us out—the ensuing journey, its challenges, hardships, and temptations to return to the old place (isn't that just what the Israelites did?)—He prepares us for the new. He takes us through the wilderness, never leaving us, constantly changing and molding us into His image, preparing us for all that he has in store.

When God told Abraham to look up, it was a holy invitation to shift his focus and embrace the promise. An invitation to look beyond the here and now, beyond the ordinary, beyond our current circumstances, toward the stunning possibilities that are only possible with Him.

Just like Mary conceived through the Holy Spirit, the Lord desires to fill us with His divine potential. But first we have to shift our focus and look away from all that holds us back.

> Let us strip off and throw aside every encumbrance (unnecessary weight) and that sin which so readily (deftly and cleverly) clings to and entangles us, and let us run with patient endurance and steady and active persistence the appointed course of the race that is set before us, looking away [from all that will distract] to Jesus, Who is the Leader and the Source of our faith (Hebrews 12:1-2 AMPC).

When we refuse to become entangled in doubt, fear, and the lies of the enemy, living our lives looking *up* instead of *at,* we will be able to embrace and run with His promises. It is then that God brings us into the place where we can glimpse our holy potential. What place? The beautiful place of promise. The place where our hearts dare to take in all He has for us, where we dare to allow it to sink in, and we dare to believe He is able and willing to bless us.

He longs for us to catch His vision for our lives—the dreams He has for us, and the future He has in store for us. He longs for us to embrace the beautiful possibilities He offers. He invites us to participate in His plans and purposes for us by grasping His promises and believing.

And that requires our hearts to come into full agreement with His.

Heart Alignment

One thing I regularly pray is for God to bring my heart into alignment with His. It's a powerful prayer I think everyone should pray daily. When our hearts are in alignment with His, we stand in the powerful position of agreement with the Sovereign King. This widens our spiritual field of vision, enabling us to see the holy possibilities. And our agreement with God's ability and promises equals unlimited potential.

I can't help but attempt to picture you, my beautiful friend, as you read this, and wonder what specific promises God has spoken to you. I'll bet God has whispered some amazing things to your heart. With everything in me, I urge you to write down His promises, pray over them, hold tight to them, and dare to believe. Believe He is able. Believe He sees your efforts and knows how hard you are working. Believe He is at work even in the hardest moments that tempt you to question everything. Believe He loves you and has good plans for you and that His heart is always, always for you. Though I may not know you personally, God does. And though I've no idea what He has promised you, I do know those promises are all *Yes* and *Amen*, because the One who promised you is faithful and able.

> All of God's promises have been fulfilled in Christ with a resounding "Yes!" And through Christ, our "Amen" (which means "Yes") ascends to God for his glory (2 Corinthians 1:20).

May the Lord enable you to continually believe. Because when we dare to believe, we will live lives of blessing that surpass our dreams in a spectacular sort of way. When doubts hammer at your heart, remember God's desire is to bless you. He is a good heavenly Father. He is faithful and trustworthy. His plans for you far exceed what you can imagine. So take courage. And dare to believe.

> So take courage! For I believe God. It will be just as He said (Acts 27:25).

Your Personal Proclamation:
SAY IT. KNOW IT. BELIEVE IT.

I will step out of the place where my circumstances have held me and look up, and I will come into agreement with and embrace the promises God offers me. I am willing to rise up out of my circumstances and to do my part. I will look beyond the here and leave my comfortable place and live out in the deep. With Him. I will dwell in the place of His blessing.

I will cultivate a willing heart that yields fully to God, along with eyes to see and recognize the blessings He has given me. I align my heart with the Lord's. I recognize that God is my shield and covering, His refreshing presence is my compensation, He strengthens and soothes me, and He blesses and rewards my efforts.

Because There's No Such Thing as Marked-Down Faith

COUNTING THE COST

Then his people believed his promises. Then they sang his praise.

PSALM 106:12

When our family relocated from Florida to Michigan due to Keith's new job, our hearts were thrilled. Adventure awaited, we were certain. And four seasons! Autumn leaves! Snow! We packed our belongings with great joy, eager to embrace this new chapter of our lives.

We left our home, barely glancing back and trusting God to sell it, even though it was empty and the holidays approached. As we drove the 1200-plus miles, our enthusiasm continued. We had purchased new coats and had them at the ready. We sang songs and talked about what we most looked forward to (sledding and ice-skating were at the very top of the list!).

When we arrived at our furnished corporate townhouse, the kids raced upstairs to lay dibs on their rooms. I walked through the downstairs, taking in our new surroundings and opening kitchen cupboards to see what I had to work with. Everything we owned, with the exception of our dog, our suitcases, and a few boxes shoved into the back of a small U-Haul trailer, was temporarily in storage until our house back in Florida sold. But we weren't worried. We trusted the Lord would work out every detail.

Yes, the start of a thing is exciting. We believe anything is possible because we believe that God guided us and will surely give us grace.

Any beginning is exciting, even fun. That's because it's easy to feel enthusiastic when troubles have not yet sullied the shiny. Before construction begins on a new building, there's often a ribbon-cutting ceremony to celebrate, with the ceremonial first shovel of dirt dug by someone wearing a suit (and sometimes heels).

Getting engaged is a thrilling time. What is more exciting than new love and the glittery promise of all your future marriage holds? And discovering a yearned-for pregnancy is such a joy. We relish creating a sweet nursery and buying adorable little outfits. We sigh dreamily as we picture our new bundle lying in the pristine (for now) crib.

Most beginnings are sparkly and enticing, surrounded by lots of hoopla. It's so easy to start a diet, an exercise routine, a daily journal, or an ambitious Bible-reading plan. We applaud each other's new goals and greet the New Year and our lofty resolutions with toasts and hearty pats on the back.

We celebrate beginnings.

But God's Word reveals that He values the opposite. In Ecclesiastes 7:8 we read that the *end* of a thing is actually *better* than the beginning.

But why are endings better than beginnings? It's hardly that beginnings don't matter. Clearly, there is no ending if we never start. In fact, Zechariah 4:10 shows us that the Lord rejoices when we stride forward in obedience and courage, however small that first step. "Do not despise these small beginnings, for the LORD rejoices to see the work begin."

So even humble beginnings matter, because it is those first, small steps that mark the beginning of our obedience and hope and give God something to work with. How can He bless something we haven't even begun? How can He equip us with grace if we haven't yet stepped out? Our initial steps, however halting and tentative, put our *Yes* into action and bring us into agreement with His plans.

So why *are* endings better? Why does God value endings so highly?

Because when we see things through to the end, we grow in patience. And reaching the end means we've endured, we've persevered, we've refused to quit. The end means we've pressed on to overcome obstacles, discouragement, and disappointments. This can only happen through steadfast endurance, which enables us to accomplish God's will and receive His promise.

> You have need of steadfast patience and endurance, so that you may perform and fully accomplish the will of God, and thus receive and carry away [and enjoy to the full] what is promised (Hebrews 10:36 AMPC).

For believers, it means we accomplished, by God's effusive grace, His purposes for that particular task and season in our lives. And it gives us divine assurance that one day we will distinctly hear the glorious words our hearts long for: "Well done, my good and faithful servant."

Yet finishing well is not easy. In fact, frequently we face fierce opposition.

When Opposition Hits Hard

Remember the old Road Runner cartoons? Back in the day, this Saturday morning staple never failed to entertain my siblings and me. The clever, super-speedy Road Runner always managed to outsmart his arch nemesis, that scoundrel Wile E. Coyote, who was constantly out to get the innocent Road Runner. Thanks to the swift bird's ingenious ways, old Wile E.'s evil plans regularly backfired on him. He bore the brunt of many an anvil, barrels of Acme dynamite, or good old-fashioned boulders.

We'd laugh when Wile E. Coyote got clobbered every week. Poor old Wile E.'s body would zigzag like an accordion, or his head would disappear down between his shoulders, or he'd get flattened like a sheet of paper. He'd be down for the count, but due to the magic of cartoon world, he ultimately managed to emerge unscathed. His accordion body straightened out, his sunken head popped back up, and his utterly flattened physique reinflated once again.

After a thorough touring of our new, temporary home, we all headed outside toward the parking lot, where our van and U-Haul waited to be unloaded. Keith popped open the back of our van, and as the door swung up he grabbed a box, then changed his mind and sat on the bumper. I glanced over at him and saw a strange expression on his face. He looked as weary and overwhelmed as I felt. I sat down next to him, then noticed he was starting to tear up. Suddenly, my eyes were brimming too.

Exhausted and overwhelmed, the stark reality of what we had done crashed down on us. We had left the safety and comfort of a beautiful home, family, friends, and all we knew, and now here we were in a strange city, in a far-flung northern state. Suddenly, it felt like we landed with a thud, and the impact made our knees and hearts tremble. As Keith and I sat there sniffling and wiping our eyes, Joshua and Emily saw us, and all of a sudden they started crying too. Great. Our entire family was now in tears. What kind of adventure was this anyway?

Fears I hadn't even considered now bubbled up from my heart into my brain. What if our house back in Florida didn't sell? What if we couldn't find a church? What if Keith hated his new job? Yes, my sister lived an hour away, but other than that, we didn't know a soul.

The first thing my overwhelmed heart and emotions wanted to do was quit. Just toss in the towel and head back home. This whole move— the one that had so excited us—now seemed risky and not worth it. I could feel my faith and heart wilt. And if the sniffling around me was any indication, my entire family felt the same way.

Sometimes the opposition hits hard.

Even though I sensed a holy drumroll when we decided to move, that didn't mean obstacles were not on the horizon. Sometimes when a door of opportunity opens up for us, the enemy takes notice. God swings the doors wide open, we walk through them in obedience, and then—*bam!*

> A wide door of opportunity for effectual [service] has opened to me [there, a great and promising one], and [there are] many adversaries (1 Corinthians 16:9 AMPC).

God had opened a door for us to relocate, but clearly there were many adversaries. I already faced my own doubts and insecurities. I regularly dealt, as we all do, with the daily interruptions of life, along with the serious concerns, health issues, and situations of friends and extended family members. And now this new reality shook me. I struggled with our decision and trying to trust that God was in it.

The crushing weight in my heart felt overwhelming. The apostle Paul penned similar words when he and Timothy endured intense trials in the province of Asia:

> We were crushed and overwhelmed beyond our ability to endure, and we thought we would never live through it. In fact, we expected to die (2 Corinthians 1:8-9).

Have you been there? Are you there now? The place of overwhelming uncertainty? This, I have learned, is a place where every woman who dares to believe must eventually walk.

And it is the perfect place to learn to rely on God like never before, as the rest of the verse points out: "But as a result, we stopped relying on ourselves and learned to rely only on God, who raises the dead" (2 Corinthians 1:9).

When our hearts are crushed, when we're treading the water of our overwhelming circumstances until our strength is utterly spent, when our situation appears uncertain, we can depend on the One who not only raises the dead, but intervenes in the very thing that looks utterly hopeless. We learn, concretely and authentically, that God is truly our only source of hope, the only One Who is able to support us and Who can intervene.

When circumstances hurt so badly we don't know how or even *if* we'll make it through, we can seek comfort from the One who is the source of all comfort. "For the more we suffer for Christ, the more God will shower us with his comfort through Christ" (2 Corinthians 1:5).

I don't know about you, but a warm, fragrant shower after a long, hard day is exactly what I need. How much more do our hearts long for and desperately need the comfort God lovingly showers on us? All we have to do is come to Him.

Come to Me, all you who labor and are heavy-laden and
overburdened, and I will cause you to rest. [I will ease
and relieve and refresh your souls.] (Matthew 11:28-29
AMPC).

Light and Momentary, My Eye

When we face daunting circumstances, whether it's a new situation or an ongoing issue that we cannot bear to endure even another
moment, it helps to understand the sometimes achingly slow process.

Though our house back in Florida sold in December (a fact, our
Realtor had pointed out back in October, that was unlikely to occur),
and we were able to close on a new house at the end of January, moving to a new state in the dead of winter was hard. On top of that, Keith
and I hit a major marriage road bump. Our entire family faced significant adjustments, sickness, and loneliness until we (finally!) met one
of our neighbors.

Without a close friend I could trust and share with, I had to believe
that God would intervene in our marriage (again) and provide godly
friendships and relationships for us all. I had to trust that this was not
all a gigantic mistake. Keith and I did receive counseling, and slowly,
gradually, after many months of praying and searching, we found a
new church, made a couple of friends, found a home school group, and
began settling in to our new lives.

Change is often Crock-Pot slow, and if you're anything like me,
you'd prefer it can-opener quick. I'm the absolute queen of wanting it
yesterday, but I have learned that God's way, even though it can often
feel like slow motion, is far better than anything I can manipulate or
force, and the *only* way that brings peace.

God is far more interested in the development of our faith and
character than in performing genie-like spectacular events that result
in a life of utopian ease. We must keep in mind that the situation(s) we
are facing are brief and fleeting. The things we cannot necessarily see
(our character development, being changed from glory to glory, Christ
increasing in us) are everlasting.

> We do not become discouraged (utterly spiritless, exhausted,
> and wearied out through fear). Though our outer man is
> [progressively] decaying and wasting away, yet our inner
> self is being [progressively] renewed day after day. For our
> light, momentary affliction (this slight distress of the pass-
> ing hour) is ever more and more abundantly preparing
> and producing and achieving for us an everlasting weight
> of glory [beyond all measure, excessively surpassing all
> comparisons and all calculations, a vast and transcendent
> glory and blessedness never to cease!] 2 Corinthians 4:16-
> 17 AMPC).

There are days (okay, weeks, months, even years!) when my prob-
lems, my situations, the flat ugly staring me in the face feel anything
but light and momentary. They feel heavy and taxing and discourag-
ing. Yet these very things—the hard things, the ugly things, the at times
unbearable things that God allows into our lives—are inexplicably at
work in us, accomplishing within us a glorious, eternal transformation.

It's not all for nothing!

And the thing we must do is the thing we want to do least of all:
Embrace it. Embrace the process, surrender to it, understanding that
God is at work and that nothing good comes without a price.

I'm convinced the hardest thing we will ever do on this earth is to
firmly grasp our God-given promises and our faith, refusing to surrender them on the altar of reality-based excuses. And reality gives us
plenty of excuses. Legitimate ones.

This is where counting the cost becomes real. Are we willing to pay
the price to accomplish all God's purposes? Are we willing to yield our
rights? Are we willing to surrender our legitimate excuses? Are we willing to pay the high cost of holding staunchly to our purposes?

Ready, Set, Bam!

After we begin pursuing the very thing God has called us to do, or
we perhaps become aware of a worrisome situation and consider our
response (and let's face it, as long as we reside this side of eternity we
will learn of many, many situations that cause concern), the first thing

we should do is pray. It's what Nehemiah, the governor of Judah (under Artaxerxes I of Persia), did when he received the devastating news that Jerusalem's wall was broken down and its gates destroyed (Nehemiah 1:3-11). In his grief, he prayed and asked the Lord for favor, since a plan was already unfolding in his heart; God was already preparing Nehemiah for a new assignment.

The second thing we should do is brace ourselves spiritually. This means we anticipate that when we step forward, there is a high chance of opposition. This is not a gloom and doom *the devil is picking on me* whine-fest, but rather a sober acknowledgment of a spiritual truth: We have an enemy, and he watches for the opportunity to pounce.

> Be well balanced (temperate, sober of mind), be vigilant and cautious at all times; for that enemy of yours, the devil, roams around like a lion roaring [in fierce hunger], seeking someone to seize upon and devour (1 Peter 5:8 AMPC).

Do we honestly think that when God gives us an assignment—whether it is a massive step of faith, a seemingly small obedience, bravely standing firm, or any of a thousand things God might lead us to but always entails daring to believe Him—that the enemy is going to roll out a red carpet? Do we think that because our assignment comes from God that the forces of hell will step back, and with a grand bow, wave us forward? *She's on a mission from God; we don't dare disturb her.*

Hardly.

When we begin to partner with the Lord and work on a specific assignment or on the different areas of our lives that He pinpoints for that specific season and time, the enemy immediately sets out to oppose us. His plan? To impede every step of progress we attempt. Satan wants us to remain a hot mess.

When we decide to start memorizing Scripture, distractions will bombard us. When we choose to work specifically on a certain personal issue, like cultivating gratitude, we'll discover loads to complain about. When we step out to lead a Bible study group, our family suddenly becomes sick. Or when we determine to read a solid book on spiritual growth, a new television show will practically shout our name.

When Nehemiah set out to rebuild Jerusalem's walls, he did so with God's blessing and the king's help. Yet right away his enemies noticed, and they were exceedingly distressed (Nehemiah 2:10). As Nehemiah's plans began to materialize, and the enemy became aware of his progress, the onslaught began.

> But when Sanballat, Tobiah, and Geshem the Arab heard of our plan, they scoffed contemptuously. "What are you doing? Are you rebelling against the king?" they asked (Nehemiah 2:19).

When we partner with the Lord, rebuilding our lives so they more accurately encompass and reflect all that God originally intended, as Nehemiah did, the enemy often lambastes us. His aim? That in scoffing at our efforts he might make us question what we're doing, causing us to doubt not only our abilities (and even our motives), but God's.

The enemy notices our progress and targets us. He batters us with lies, intimidation, and discouragement. He wants us to doubt God's promises, doubt the legitimacy of the work we are involved in, and doubt God's provision and ability to strengthen us and work in and through us.

Reality Check 101

My husband, Keith, has mad sale-finding skills. If you need it, he can likely find it on clearance, buy-one-get-one, or so seriously marked down it'll make you jump for joy. Anyone who knows Keith realizes that if they're in the market for a new item, all they need to do is mention it to my hubby because the man can chase down a bargain like nobody's business.

And who doesn't love a deal? I rarely buy anything unless it's on sale. I figure full price is for rich people, so let them have the honors.

Do we likewise think of faith as something we might attain with the least possible payout? Is faith a cheap commodity? Is it a mere nod of assent, a quiet prayer, and then living happily ever after? Does faith go on sale? Is it ever marked down? When Jesus Himself admonishes us to count the cost, do we? "But don't begin until you count the cost.

For who would begin construction of a building without first calculating the cost to see if there is enough money to finish it?" (Luke 14:28).

Do we pause to consider what this verse actually means and how it might apply to us? Do we stop and think that things might not go as easily as we prefer (in fact, we're pretty much guaranteed they won't)? Believing God's promises could cost us absolutely everything.

How can we possibly hope to acquire at the discount of ease that for which Jesus paid so dearly? Do we value our relative comfort above what is actually required to attain and work out our promises—indeed our very faith—with fear and trembling?

> As you have always obeyed [my suggestions], so now, not only [with the enthusiasm you would show] in my presence but much more because I am absent, *work out (cultivate, carry out to the goal, and fully complete) your own salvation with reverence and awe and trembling* (self-distrust, with serious caution, tenderness of conscience, watchfulness against temptation, timidly shrinking from whatever might offend God and discredit the name of Christ) (Philippians 2:12 AMPC, italics mine).

If we want to be women who dare to believe God, should not we then guard against the very slothfulness and pride that indubitably prevent us from finishing well? Should we not consider those who have gone before us, paying an unimaginable price as they dared to believe in spite of the horrific?

What about those who were tortured, jeered at, and had their backs whipped? What of those who were destitute and oppressed and mistreated? What of those who were chained in prisons, died by stoning, or were literally sawed in half (see Hebrews 11:35-38)?

Hebrews 11 cuts through our bargain-faith mentality. Because bargain faith is fake faith. Marked-down faith is no faith at all. It's a lazy faith born of either convenience or crisis. It's an insult to the One Who paid the highest imaginable price.

But we yearn to be women of valor, and we are when we count the cost and refuse to give up, back down, cave in, or freak out (for long).

When we don't yield to fear or panic. When we don't allow ourselves to be disturbed by what we see. Talk about a perspective shift!

Hebrews 11 challenges us. It changes us from proud and entitled women to humble and grateful women. It provides the divine perspective we desperately need when we're counting the cost. Scripture declares that these particular heroes of the faith were "men of whom the world was not worthy" (Hebrews 11:38 AMPC). Those eight words reverberate through my heart. They implore us to live our lives in His honor, in a manner worthy of the Lord.

> That you may walk (live and conduct yourselves) in a manner worthy of the Lord, fully pleasing to Him and desiring to please Him in all things, bearing fruit in every good work and steadily growing and increasing in and by the knowledge of God [with fuller, deeper, and clearer insight, acquaintance, and recognition] (Colossians 1:10 AMPC).

As the apostle Paul wrote to and prayed for the Colossian people, his words reflect God's will for us as we walk out our faith in the hardest of seasons in a manner that pleases God. Regardless of the cost.

In spite of the opposition, Nehemiah's work continued. A large group of devoted, hardworking men worked side by side, building various gates, setting up the doors, and working on different sections of the wall (see Nehemiah, chapter three).

But Nehemiah's enemies continued to relentlessly harass him and oppose his work. It would have been so easy to wait it out. To take a break until Sanballat, Tobiah, and their motley crew of opposition were out of the picture. Yet, Nehemiah refused to quit. He refused to allow the enemy to dictate his response and stop his work. He refused to wait for optimal conditions.

We cannot wait for conditions to be perfect. Such thinking is a lie and a trap. We live in an imperfect world; the enemy has influence and, unfortunately, our circumstances will never, ever be perfect. That means we begin when God tells us to begin, not when every situation, everyone, and everything in our lives is absolutely, undeniably peachy.

Scripture tells us when we wait for all conditions to be favorable, we will not sow, and we will not reap. (Not good.) "He who observes the wind [and waits for all conditions to be favorable] will not sow, and he who regards the clouds will not reap" (Ecclesiastes 11:4 AMPC).

Instead, we should live poised to take action when God makes it clear to us. That's an inward stance. We are poised to move when God leads us. We don't flinch, and we don't stop when circumstances attempt to derail us. We are led by the Holy Spirit. If God says yield, we yield. If He says wait, we wait. And if He says full steam ahead, then baby, we go.

Nehemiah wasn't swayed by the opposition. And we shouldn't be either.

We also cannot be surprised by our less-than-stellar circumstances. I'm so guilty of this. I want my life to hum along in a nonstop, pleasant vibe, and unless cake and friends are involved, I don't care for surprises. Especially unpleasant surprises. Yet nearly every time something hard happens, bingo (you guessed it), I'm shocked. You'd think by now I'd know better. Especially because Scripture reminds us not to be surprised when we face the crazy, the awful, the downright devastating. "Dear friends, don't be surprised at the fiery trials you are going through, as if something strange were happening to you" (1 Peter 4:12).

Instead, we're told to be glad. Actually, *very glad*. I don't know many people (or anyone) who receives bad news and is instantly very glad. Yet there it is, in the very next verse:

> Instead, be very glad—for these trials make you partners with Christ in his suffering, so that you will have the wonderful joy of seeing his glory when it is revealed to all the world (1 Peter 4:13).

It's not necessary to be glad for the trials themselves, but for what they indicate and what they accomplish. Every rough situation, all the opposition, and every bit of heartache makes us partners with Jesus. And as His partners, we will one day see unimaginable realms of His glory.

Though Sanballat's unexpected attack hit hard, Nehemiah didn't allow it to knock him off kilter. He kept right on working.. Even when Sanballat flew into a rage and ridiculed the Jews (Nehemiah 4:1).

Nothing angers the enemy more than when we begin rebuilding. And *all* of God's work involves rebuilding. It matters not what is being rebuilt. If God is the architect behind it (and He is), then the enemy does not like it—will not stand for it and becomes enraged over it. What's more, the enemy minimizes our efforts, mocking us. He targets and attacks our efforts.

> Do they actually think they can make something of stones from a rubbish heap—and charred ones at that? (Nehemiah 4:2).

Do they actually think?

The enemy still uses the same familiar taunts. *Do you actually think you can make something of your life? Do you actually think you can make something of your marriage? Do you actually think you can make something of this dream of yours?*

What the enemy is essentially saying is, *Who do you think you are? Look at you! You're no better than rubbish. You're a worthless, useless, scorched stone.*

The enemy fails to understand a twofold truth: What we think matters because as Scripture reminds us, "For as he thinks in his heart, so is he" (Proverbs 23:7 AMPC).

As women who dare to believe, we must recognize that the enemy will oppose our work, and he won't fight fair. He will insult us, demean us, and belittle us. It matters not. We know who we are. We know Whose we are. The enemy opposes the rebuilding of our hearts and lives. We must learn to not only discern his attempts to discourage us, but, like Nehemiah, to resist them and continue working anyway.

And the other half of the twofold truth: Yes, actually, we *do* dare to think we can make something of our lives. Just stop, breathe in that thought, and say it out loud. Yes, right now. *I dare to think I can make something of my life.* Well done!

But not in our own strength. Never in our own strength. When we are busy with the Lord's work, He is the One who supernaturally equips us. He is the One who enables us. Philippians 2:13 (AMPC) says, "[Not in your own strength] for it is God Who is all the while effectually at work in you [energizing and creating in you the power and desire], both to will and to work for His good pleasure and satisfaction and delight."

God plucks us out of the rubbish heap, and He doesn't consider us disqualified or useless or worthless. Isaiah 64:8 points out, "We all are formed by your hand." All pottery goes into the fire. All of it. It is not useful to the potter until it reaches the necessary temperature for the clay to be cured. Hardened. Useful.

What Sanballat and his cohorts didn't understand then, and what the enemy still doesn't get, is that God uses scorched stones. Every one of us who have withstood the fire of adversity can, like Nehemiah, take courage, knowing it is God Himself who rescues us out of the rubbish heap. He rescues us and places us exactly where He wants. He doesn't use perfect stones because—news flash!—there aren't any!

After the enemy's mockery, Nehemiah responded in a remarkable manner. He didn't engage with Sanballat. He didn't haul off and lob him with a rock. He didn't threaten him if he wouldn't stop. He did something far more effective.

He prayed.

Because of that prayer, more progress happened, and (of course) the enemy became more angry. Sanballat and his cronies then plotted together to fight and make Nehemiah fail. "And they all plotted together to come and fight against Jerusalem, to injure and cause confusion and failure in it" (Nehemiah 4:8 AMPC).

It was a last-ditch effort to stop Nehemiah's progress. But it didn't work because Nehemiah and his people armed themselves two ways: with prayer and with weapons. On and on it went, the progress and the opposition. But the things that carried Nehemiah and the people through to the end turned out to be the same thing each one of us can do: We can pray, and we can arm ourselves through Scripture and worship. Then we can imprint the Lord on our hearts, take courage from Him, and fight!

> I looked [them over] and rose up and said to the nobles
> and officials and the other people, Do not be afraid of the
> enemy; [earnestly] remember the Lord and imprint Him
> [on your minds], great and terrible, and [take from Him
> courage to] fight for your brethren, your sons, your daugh-
> ters, your wives, and your homes (Nehemiah 4:14 AMPC).

When we focus on God's greatness, the enemy's true, miniscule size and feeble ability becomes clear to us. When we draw our courage from the Lord, He enables us to do our part—to stand, to work, and to fight.

Another key to embracing God's promises and counting the cost isn't difficult to decipher. We *can* keep believing in spite of what we see. It's exactly what Nehemiah and the Jewish people did. "We also pray that you will be strengthened with all his glorious power so you will have all the endurance and patience you need" (Colossians 1:11).

It is God's glorious power that gives us every last ounce of endurance and patience our hearts require.

> Do not be afraid, for I have ransomed you. I have called
> you by name; you are mine. When you go through deep
> waters, I will be with you. When you go through rivers of
> difficulty, you will not drown. When you walk through the
> fire of oppression, you will not be burned up; the flames
> will not consume you. For I am the LORD, your God, the
> Holy One of Israel, your Savior (Isaiah 43:1-3).

When enemy opposition hits hard, and we feel flattened beneath the weight of the attack, God removes the boulder and restores us. He reflates our deflated hearts.

God uses scorched stones.

We make the holy decision to dig in, remain committed, to see things through to the end, to hang in there because obedience is where the blessing is. We set our faces like flint (Isaiah 50:7).

How We End Matters

How many times do we start with a bang and end with a whimper? How often do we give up before we've really gotten started? How many times has God spoken specifically and radically to our hearts, stirring and filling us with certainty and purpose and great joy...only to lose sight of the finish line because discouragement hits and the reality of difficult circumstances (or even just regular old life) interrupts?

Ending well far exceeds starting with a flourish. I am convinced that the primary key to ending well lies in the second half of the verse in Ecclesiastes, which we talked about at the very beginning of this chapter:

> Better is the end of a thing than the beginning thereof: and *the patient in spirit is better than the proud in spirit* (Ecclesiastes 7:8 KJV, italics mine).

Maybe, like me, you have always assumed that the opposite of patience is impatience. Or frustration. Or quite possibly exasperation. God knows I am expertly familiar with all three (ahem), and I'm fairly certain you just might possibly relate on some teensy scale.

Yet this verse points out that the opposite of patience is actually *pride*.

Pride fosters impatience. It leads us to sigh and inwardly complain when the checkout line is too long. Pride taps its indignant foot. Pride is always right. Pride demands.

Do we demand things go our way? Do we insist we know the right way? Do we sigh and roll our eyes when we're slowed or inconvenienced? Welcome to the Proud in Spirit Club. Our motto? *I shouldn't have to wait, and I am probably not wrong.*

It is a patient, humble woman who yields to and entrusts herself, her current hard situations, her unthinkable circumstances, and her aching disappointments to the Lord. It is a humble heart that bows, declaring, *Your will be done, oh God*, straining to believe that good will come out of what He allows for a season (Romans 8:28).

It is a humble heart that recognizes her own way isn't the best, that God's ways are higher and significantly superior than her ways.

> "My thoughts are nothing like your thoughts," says the LORD. "And my ways are far beyond anything you could imagine. For just as the heavens are higher than the earth, so my ways are higher than your ways and my thoughts higher than your thoughts" (Isaiah 55:8-9).

He is the God of everything—of the entire, vast picture—and He sees and knows matters far above our meager and limited understanding.

Authentic faith embraces every promise God offers, knowing it will cost us everything. It will cost us our ideas of security, how we think things should be, and the way we think our lives will turn out. It will cost us our pseudo-control, relinquishing our rights, and picking up our cross to follow Him. In other words, finishing well will require our very lives.

> [I assure you] by the pride which I have in you in [your fellowship and union with] Christ Jesus our Lord, that *I die daily* [I face death every day and *die to self*] (1 Corinthians 15:31 AMPC, italics mine).

Do we die daily? When the choice is excruciating pain or our own way, which do we pick? When change is achingly slow, do we calm our hearts and trust the Lord, or murmur in indignation? Do we willingly surrender our rights?

When Jesus breathed, "It is finished!" (John 19:30), He had completely fulfilled all that the Father intended. Through humiliation, scorn, unthinkable torture, and crushing heartache, He did not shrink back, run away, or change His mind.

Should our goal be any less? Should we not determine to fulfill all the Father intends for us, even when it's hard? Even when it costs us more dearly than we could ever have known?

As women who dare to believe, we want every last ounce of our willing hearts squeezed to the last drop. We want to face God assured that we willingly counted the cost, accomplished our parts, and willingly finished all He required of us.

It is my fervent prayer that each one of us will be able to say on that great day:

> I have fought the good fight, I have finished the race, and I have remained faithful (2 Timothy 4:7).

Your Personal Proclamation:
SAY IT. KNOW IT. BELIEVE IT.

I have a heart of valor, and I refuse to give up, back down, cave in, or freak out over my circumstances. I am determined to count the cost and grow in patience and humility. My heart is to consistently yield to and entrust myself and every one of my disappointments and situations to the Lord. I will trust God's timing and not demand my own way. I will live poised to take action and guard against slothfulness and pride. I will stop relying on myself and learn to rely only on God. As I count the cost and set my face like flint, I believe God will comfort me and ease and relieve and refresh my soul.

Questions for Personal Reflection or Group Study

Chapter 1—And Then I Knew *Normal* Wasn't Out of the Question

1. How do *you* define *normal*?

2. Do you sometimes try to figure out how God is going to work things out? Ask God to reveal to you times your mind has interfered with your faith, and ask Him to point out the next time you're on the verge of doing the same thing.

3. Have you ever made an official decision to do whatever it takes to believe God and cooperate with Him? Might you be willing to do that right now?

4. Do you think you need a minor remodel, tweaking, or a total (from the foundation up) do-over?

5. When was the last time it cost you to spend time with the Lord?

Chapter 2—Wait! You Mean That's Not Who I Really Am?

1. Have you ever embraced erroneous thoughts concerning yourself? Write three fresh, new, good thoughts about yourself to think instead.

2. Would you say you are more fluent in cultural lingo or Scripture?

3. Do you think you've ever accommodated a spirit of error? Ask the Holy Spirit to reveal erroneous thoughts and to help you replace them with truth.

4. What distortions or lies concerning your value might be embedded in your heart? Ask God to bring freedom and to anchor you in truth.

5. Do you feel you've ever adhered to names the Lord never intended for you (such as Insecure, Unloved, Unknown, Fearful, Doubtful, Guilty, Depressed, Anxious)? Ask God to show you your authentic name and true identity.

Chapter 3—The Part Where We Keep Going Through Hard Stuff

1. Has a Bible verse ever rubbed you the wrong way? Which one, and why?

2. Have you ever expected or desired God to excuse you from future pain?

3. Have you shared a dream with a family member or friend that was not well received?

4. Has any sort of family dysfunction ever made it feel like your circumstances own you? Have you released those heavy hurts to God?

5. Is forgiveness easy or hard for you? God gives us grace to make the choice to forgive and let go when we ask Him.

Chapter 4—The Chasm-Closer

1. What recent chasm has appeared in your life, or what large chasm have you been unable to cross?

2. Do the enemy's malicious words sometime ring true to

you? Ask the Lord to help you recognize a skewed truth so that seeds of confusion and discouragement are not planted.

3. Is your heart in tune with the Holy Spirit, so you are able to stand in faith against the enemy's propaganda?

4. Have you asked the Lord for fresh perspective of the chasm you are facing, so you can recognize God showing Himself strong?

5. When is the last time you worshipped God in the midst of your suffering?

Chapter 5—For Our Every Meltdown, Freak-Out, and Gut-Wrenching Hurt

1. Has the Holy Spirit ever disclosed to you something that was to come? If not, ask Him to make you sensitive and alert so you can recognize and take to heart His disclosures.

2. Do you lean more toward distraction or maintaining your focus? Ask the Lord to help you increase and maintain laser-like focus.

3. Do you tend to panic first and ask questions later? Pray for the ability to respond in calm wisdom.

4. Why *are* you afraid? Disclose your fears in prayer to Jesus, asking Him to help you. Remember, He is Immanuel, God with us.

5. Do you battle the what-ifs? Confess and surrender each one to the Lord, and ask Him to help you know—really know—that He is always at work.

Chapter 6—Knocking Knees Aside

1. Are you more of a brave soul, or (tell the truth) do you lean toward the cowardly?

2. Can you recall specific times fear has used bully tactics against you?

3. Are you more fluent in lie or in Scripture? Which do you more readily understand?

4. When is the last time you stood up to the enemy by remembering who you are in Christ and using your right as God's treasured daughter?

5. Which phrase do you use most? 1) I would but… or 2) I am well able! Challenge yourself to use the second phrase over and over for the next two weeks.

Chapter 7—Because Every Iota of You Matters

1. Were seeds of insignificance planted in you at some point? Or did you begin believing a specific lie about yourself?

2. Which lie most resonates with you? 1) When I Do *This* I'm Important, or 2) If I'm Busy Then I Matter.

3. Have you ever believed that you were too unimportant to be worth consideration? Ask God to help you instead know that He always hears you and values you.

4. Take a pen and write the words: *If you only knew*. Then pray and ask God to speak to your heart the private, personal thing He wants you to know concerning your sense of significance.

5. Are you in need of a new inner wardrobe? Absorb Psalm 103:4 and allow it to begin clothing you beautifully.

Chapter 8—It Shatters the Bleakest Despair

1. Have you recently visited a raw, awful place? The next time you face the exact opposite of what you hoped for, ask God for a holy awareness that He is at work, that your

hopes have been sown in order to produce a rich harvest of promise.

2. Do you tend to rehearse an incident over and over? Ask God for the holy ability to shake it off.

3. Would you like for hope to become your new default setting? Determine to practice hoping, in spite of what you see.

4. When is the last time you dared to believe that God is ultimately steering the things in your life to exactly where they (and you) need to be?

5. Do you have a Velcro heart? One that clings to the Lord and His Word?

Chapter 9—Neither Our Guilt Complex Nor Our Doubts Nor Our Catastrophic Failures Can Separate Us

1. When and where have you most experienced tangible love?

2. Do you tend to agree with the enemy's lies that you aren't lovable? Ask God to give you increased discernment so next time you will recognize and refute that lie.

3. How has God's love at work in you changed you? How is it still changing you?

4. Does God's love feel far away, or like an inviting oasis to you?

5. What excuses have you used that block your acceptance of Christ's love? (Fill in the blank: God couldn't possibly love me when I _____.) Then rip that excuse to shreds and inhale this fact: Nothing can separate me from the love of God in Christ Jesus.

Chapter 10—It's Not the CIA, but Special Assignments Abound

1. Have you buried any gifts? If you're not sure, pray. Ask God to show you.

2. Do you know what gifts God has given you? Ask Him to reveal your specific talents and gifts to you.

3. Has God ever asked you to do something for which you felt completely inadequate? Did you succumb to your feelings of inadequacy or obey anyway?

4. Have facts ever roadblocked you when you tried to step out and use your gifts? Commit 2 Corinthians 12:9 to memory.

5. Are you uncertain of what God has placed within you? Ask the Lord to show you your holy potential.

Chapter 11—It Surpasses Our Dreams in a Spectacular Sort of Way

1. Can you recall a special time God used Scripture to lift your heart?

2. Are you willing to choose to embrace God's truth and rise above the situation you're currently facing? Are you willing to embrace His blessing and the effort it will require?

3. Has God ever required you to move forward and leave some form of ugly behind?

4. When was the last time God called you out of your comfort zone? Are you willing to accept His invitation to live in the deep?

5. Is your heart in alignment with God's? Determine to pray daily for your heart to come into alignment with God's.

Chapter 12—Because There's No Such Thing as Marked-Down Faith

1. Has opposition hit you hard? Commit 2 Corinthians 1:9 to memory.

2. Are you willing to embrace the undesirable things God has allowed into your life? Pray for an enduring heart that recognizes God is accomplishing glorious, eternal things in you.

3. Do you value comfort over what is required to attain God's promises to you? Pray for the ability to guard against desiring a life of ease.

4. Have you ever started a new project or goal with a bang and then ended with a fizzle? What happened?

5. Are you willing to die daily? To trust the Lord without murmuring? Ask Him to help you fight the good fight, to finish the race, to keep the faith.

Supernaturally Stabilizing Scriptures

He alone is my rock and my salvation, my fortress where I will not be shaken (Psalm 62:6).

The [uncompromisingly] righteous shall flourish like the palm tree [be long-lived, stately, upright, useful, and fruitful]; they shall grow like a cedar in Lebanon [majestic, stable, durable, and incorruptible] (Psalm 92:12 AMPC).

For from of old no one has heard nor perceived by the ear, nor has the eye seen a God besides You, Who works and shows Himself active on behalf of him who [earnestly] waits for Him (Isaiah 64:4 AMPC).

Let us therefore, receiving a kingdom that is firm and stable and cannot be shaken, offer to God pleasing service and acceptable worship, with modesty and pious care and godly fear and awe (Hebrews 12:28 AMPC).

I have set the Lord continually before me; because He is at my right hand, I shall not be moved (Psalm 16:8 AMPC).

I have told you these things, so that in Me you may have [perfect] peace and confidence. In the world you have tribulation and trials and distress and frustration; but be of good cheer [take courage; be confident, certain, undaunted]! For I have overcome the world. [*I have deprived it of power to harm you* and have conquered it for you.] (John 16:33 AMPC, italics mine).

The Lord is my Strength and my [impenetrable] Shield; my heart trusts in, relies on, and confidently leans on Him, and I am helped; therefore my heart greatly rejoices, and with my song will I praise Him (Psalm 28:7 AMPC).

For our light, momentary affliction (this slight distress of the passing hour) is ever more and more abundantly pre-paring and producing and achieving for us an everlasting weight of glory [beyond all measure, excessively surpassing all comparisons and all calculations, a vast and transcen-dent glory and blessedness never to cease!] (2 Corinthians 4:17 AMPC).

Promises for a Hot Mess

I will make you whole.

- So if the Son liberates you [makes you free men], then you are really and unquestionably free (John 8:36 AMPC).

- And I will restore or replace for you the years that the locust has eaten—the hopping locust, the stripping locust, and the crawling locust (Joel 2:25 AMPC).

- And he said unto her, Daughter, thy faith hath made thee whole; go in peace, and be whole of thy plague (Mark 5:34 KJV).

I will give you a new identity.

- Don't copy the behavior and customs of this world, but let God transform you into a new person by changing the way you think. Then you will learn to know God's will for you, which is good and pleasing and perfect (Romans 12:2).

- You are precious to me. You are honored, and I love you (Isaiah 43:4).

- I am my lover's, and my lover is mine (Song of Songs 6:3).

I will work all things for good.

- Fear not [there is nothing to fear], for I am with you; do not look around you in terror and be dismayed, for I am your God. I will strengthen and harden you to difficulties, yes, I will help you; yes, I will hold you up and retain you

with My [victorious] right hand of rightness and justice
(Isaiah 41:10 AMPC).

- My times are in Your hands; deliver me from the hands
of my foes and those who pursue me and persecute me
(Psalm 31:15 AMPC).

- And we know that God causes everything to work together
for the good of those who love God and are called according to his purpose for them (Romans 8:28).

I will enable you.

- I will cry to God Most High, Who performs on my behalf
and rewards me [Who brings to pass His purposes for me
and surely completes them]! (Psalm 57:2 AMPC).

- [Not in your own strength] for it is God Who is all the
while effectually at work in you [energizing and creating
in you the power and desire], both to will and to work for
His good pleasure and satisfaction and delight (Philippians
2:13 AMPC).

- The eyes of the LORD search the whole earth in order to
strengthen those whose hearts are fully committed to him
(2 Chronicles 16:9).

I AM your stability.

- Peace I leave with you; My [own] peace I now give and
bequeath to you. Not as the world gives do I give to you.
Do not let your hearts be troubled, neither let them be
afraid. [Stop allowing yourselves to be agitated and disturbed; and do not permit yourselves to be fearful and
intimidated and cowardly and unsettled.] (John 14:27
AMPC).

- Blessed (happy, fortunate, to be envied) is the man whom

You discipline and instruct, O Lord, and teach out of Your law. That You may give him power to keep himself calm in the days of adversity, until the [inevitable] pit of corruption is dug for the wicked (Psalm 94:12-13 AMPC).

- Cast your burden on the Lord [releasing the weight of it] and He will sustain you; He will never allow the [consistently] righteous to be moved (made to slip, fall, or fail) (Psalm 55:22 AMPC).

You are brave.

- For God did not give us a spirit of timidity (of cowardice, of craven and cringing and fawning fear), but [He has given us a spirit] of power and of love and of calm and well-balanced mind and discipline and self-control (2 Timothy 1:7 AMPC).
- The LORD is on my side; I will not fear (Psalm 118:6 KJV).
- She is clothed with strength and dignity, and she laughs without fear of the future (Proverbs 31:25).

You are significant.

- LORD, you have examined my heart and know everything about me. You know when I sit down or stand up. You know my thoughts even when I'm far away (Psalm 139:1-2).
- And therefore the Lord [earnestly] waits [expecting, looking, and longing] to be gracious to you; and therefore He lifts Himself up, that He may have mercy on you and show loving-kindness to you. For the Lord is a God of justice. Blessed (happy, fortunate, to be envied) are all those who [earnestly] wait for Him, who expect and look and long for Him [for His victory, His favor, His love, His peace, His

joy, and His matchless, unbroken companionship] (Isaiah 30:18 AMPC).

- For the Lord takes pleasure in His people; He will beautify the humble with salvation and adorn the wretched with victory (Psalm 149:4 AMPC).

I will give you hope.

- Wait and hope for and expect the Lord; be brave and of good courage and let your heart be stout and enduring. Yes, wait for and hope for and expect the Lord (Psalm 27:14 AMPC).
- May the God of your hope so fill you with all joy and peace in believing [through the experience of your faith] that by the power of the Holy Spirit you may abound and be overflowing (bubbling over) with hope (Romans 15:13 AMPC).
- But I will hope continually, and will praise You yet more and more (Psalm 71:14 AMPC).

I will give you My unfailing love.

- Surely your goodness and unfailing love will pursue me all the days of my life, and I will live in the house of the LORD forever (Psalm 23:6).
- See how very much our Father loves us, for he calls us his children, and that is what we are! (1 John 3:1).
- He brought me to the banqueting house, and his banner over me was love [for love waved as a protecting and comforting banner over my head when I was near him] (Song of Solomon 2:4 AMPC).

You are a woman of destiny.

- For God's gifts and His call are irrevocable. [He never withdraws them when once they are given, and He does not change His mind about those to whom He gives His grace or to whom He sends His call.] (Romans 11:29 AMPC).

- You saw me before I was born. Every day of my life was recorded in your book. Every moment was laid out before a single day had passed (Psalm 139:16).

- For we are God's [own] handiwork (His workmanship), recreated in Christ Jesus, [born anew] that we may do those good works which God predestined (planned beforehand) for us [taking paths which He prepared ahead of time], that we should walk in them [living the good life which He prearranged and made ready for us to live] (Ephesians 2:10 AMPC).

I will bless you.

- Fear not, Abram, I am your Shield, your abundant compensation, and your reward shall be exceedingly great (Genesis 15:1 AMPC).

- For You send blessings of good things to meet him; You set a crown of pure gold on his head (Psalm 21:3 AMPC).

- And God will generously provide all you need. Then you will always have everything you need and plenty left over to share with others (2 Corinthians 9:8).

Counting the cost. You can!

- For the more we suffer for Christ, the more God will shower us with his comfort through Christ (2 Corinthians 1:5).

- Therefore we do not become discouraged (utterly spirit-
less, exhausted, and wearied out through fear). Though our
outer man is [progressively] decaying and wasting away,
yet our inner self is being [progressively] renewed day after
day. For our light, momentary affliction (this slight distress of the passing hour) is ever more and more abundantly preparing and producing and achieving for us an
everlasting weight of glory [beyond all measure, excessively
surpassing all comparisons and all calculations, a vast and
transcendent glory and blessedness never to cease!],
(2 Corinthians 4:16-17 AMPC).

- Because the Sovereign LORD helps me, I will not be
disgraced. Therefore, I have set my face like a stone,
determined to do his will. And I know that I will not be
put to shame (Isaiah 50:7).

Also from Julie Gillies

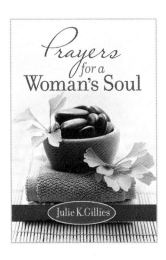

Women have a prayer list a mile long: Husbands. Children. Friends. Church leaders. Neighborhood situations. The military. World events. The sick and the shut-in and the chronically struggling. With so much on their minds, it's no wonder that women sometimes forget to pray for themselves, neglecting their own needs and spiritual growth.

Prayers for a Woman's Soul is for every woman who specializes in "front-burner prayer," praying for whatever is boiling over at the moment (and there's always something boiling over!). This inspiring book will teach wives, mothers, friends, sisters, and daughters how to cover themselves with prayer on a regular basis. Each devotion includes powerful spiritual insight, personalized Scripture, and a prayer to help begin the conversation with God. This soul-pampering journey will rejuvenate, refresh, and revive a woman's soul!

Julie K. Gillies is the author of *Prayers for a Woman's Soul*. Healed from a traumatic childhood and awed that God saved her seriously troubled marriage, Julie refreshes and strengthens others with her words. She and her husband, Keith, have three adult children and four grandchildren.

To learn more about Julie K. Gillies
or to read sample chapters,
visit our website:
www.harvesthousepublishers.com

To learn more about Harvest House books and
to read sample chapters, visit our website:

www.harvesthousepublishers.com

HARVEST HOUSE PUBLISHERS
EUGENE, OREGON